THE
CHRISTIAN
NEW
YEAR

THE AWAKENING CALENDAR

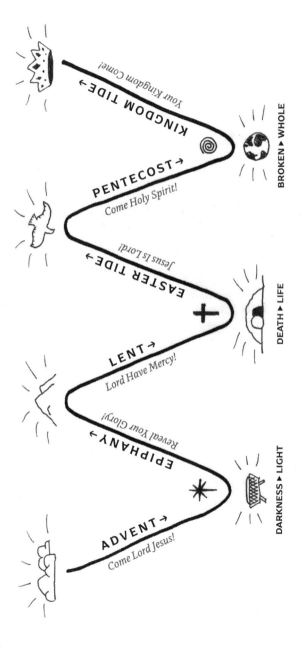

ADVENT →
Come Lord Jesus!

EPIPHANY ←
Reveal Your Glory!

LENT →
Lord Have Mercy!

EASTER TIDE ←
Jesus Is Lord!

PENTECOST →
Come Holy Spirit!

KINGDOM TIDE ←
Your Kingdom Come!

DARKNESS ▶ LIGHT

DEATH ▶ LIFE

BROKEN ▶ WHOLE

The Seedbed Daily Text

THE
CHRISTIAN
NEW
YEAR

Advent

J. D. WALT

Scripture quotations are taken from New Revised Standard Version Bible, copyright © 1989 National Council of the Churches of Christ in the United States of America. Used by permission. All rights reserved.

Scripture quotations marked NIV are taken from THE HOLY BIBLE, NEW INTERNATIONAL VERSION®, NIV® Copyright © 1973, 1978, 1984, 2011 by Biblica, Inc.™ Used by permission. All rights reserved worldwide.

Scripture quotations marked ESV are from The Holy Bible, English Standard Version® copyright © 2001 by Crossway, a publishing ministry of Good News Publishers. Used by permission. All rights reserved.

Printed in the United States of America

Cover and page design by Strange Last Name
Page layout by PerfecType, Nashville, Tennessee

Walt, John David.
  The Christian new year : Advent / J.D. Walt. – Franklin, Tennessee : Seedbed Publishing, ©2020.

      pages ; cm. -- (The Seedbed daily text)

      ISBN 9781628247985 (paperback)
      ISBN 9781628248043 (Mobi)
      ISBN 9781628248050 (ePub)
      ISBN 9781628248067 (uPDF)

      1. Advent--Prayers and devotions. 2. Advent--Meditations.
      3. Devotional calendars. I. Title. II. Series

BV40.W342 2020   242/.332   2020943800

SEEDBED PUBLISHING
Franklin, Tennessee
seedbed.com

Contents

An Invitation to Awakening

This resource comes with an invitation.

The invitation is as simple as it is comprehensive. It is not an invitation to commit your life to this or that cause or to join an organization or to purchase another book. The invitation is this: to wake up to the life you always hoped was possible and the reason you were put on planet Earth.

It begins with following Jesus Christ. In case you are unaware, Jesus was born in the first century BCE into a poor family from Nazareth, a small village located in what is modern-day Israel. While his birth was associated with extraordinary phenomena, we know little about his childhood. At approximately thirty years of age, Jesus began a public mission of preaching, teaching, and healing throughout the region known as Galilee. His mission was characterized by miraculous signs and wonders; extravagant care of the poor and marginalized; and multiple unconventional claims about his own identity and purpose. In short, he claimed to be the incarnate Son of God with the mission and power to save people from sin, deliver them from death, and bring them into the now and eternal kingdom of God—on earth as it is in heaven.

In the spring of his thirty-third year, during the Jewish Passover celebration, Jesus was arrested by the religious authorities, put on trial in the middle of the night, and at their urging, sentenced to death by a Roman governor. On the day known to history as Good Friday, Jesus was crucified on a Roman cross. He was buried in a borrowed tomb. On the following Sunday, according to multiple eyewitness accounts, he was physically raised from the dead. He appeared to hundreds of people, taught his disciples, and prepared for what was to come.

Forty days after the resurrection, Jesus ascended bodily into the heavens where, according to the Bible, he sits at the right hand of God, as the Lord of heaven and earth. Ten days after his ascension, in a gathering of more than three thousand people on the day of Pentecost, a Jewish day of celebration, something truly extraordinary happened. A loud and powerful wind swept over the people gathered. Pillars of what appeared to be fire descended upon the followers of Jesus. The Holy Spirit, the presence and power of God, filled the people, and the church was born. After this, the followers of Jesus went forth and began to do the very things Jesus did—preaching, teaching, and healing; planting churches and making disciples all over the world. Today, more than two thousand years later, the movement has reached us. This is the Great Awakening and it has never stopped.

Yes, two thousand years hence and more than two billion followers of Jesus later, this awakening movement of Jesus Christ and his church stands stronger than ever. Billions of ordinary people the world over have discovered in Jesus Christ an awakened life they never imagined possible. They have overcome challenges, defeated addictions, endured untenable hardships and suffering with unexplainable joy, and stared death in the face with the joyful confidence of eternal life. They have healed the sick, gathered the outcasts, embraced the oppressed, loved the poor, contended for justice, labored for peace, cared for the dying, and, yes, even raised the dead.

We all face many challenges and problems. They are deeply personal, yet when joined together, they create enormous and complex chaos in the world, from our hearts to our homes to our churches and our cities. All of this chaos traces to two originating problems: sin and death. Sin, far beyond mere moral failure, describes the fundamental broken condition of every human being. Sin separates us from God and others, distorts and destroys our deepest identity as the image-bearers of God, and poses a fatal problem from which we cannot save ourselves. It results in an ever-diminishing quality of life and ultimately ends in eternal death. Because Jesus lived a life of sinless perfection, he is able to save us from sin and restore us to a right relationship with God, others, and ourselves. He did this through his sacrificial death on the cross on our behalf. Because Jesus rose from the dead, he is able to deliver us from death and bring us into a quality of life both eternal and unending.

This is the gospel of Jesus Christ: pardon from the penalty of sin, freedom from the power of sin, deliverance from the grip of death, and awakening to the supernatural empowerment of the Holy Spirit to live powerfully for the good of others and for the glory of God. Jesus asks only that we acknowledge our broken selves as failed sinners, trust him as our Savior, and follow him as our Lord. Following Jesus does not mean an easy life; however, it does lead to a life of power and purpose, joy in the face of suffering, and profound, even world-changing, love for God and people.

All of this is admittedly a lot to take in. Remember, this is an invitation. Will you follow Jesus? Don't let the failings of his followers deter you. Come and see for yourself.

Here's a prayer to get you started:

> Our Father in heaven, it's me (say your name). I want to know you. I want to live an awakened life. I confess I am a sinner. I have failed myself, others, and you in many ways. I know you made me for a purpose, and I want to fulfill that purpose with my one life. I want to follow Jesus Christ. Jesus, thank you for the gift of your life and death and resurrection and ascension on my behalf. I want to walk in relationship with you as Savior and Lord. Would you lead me into the fullness and newness of life I was made for? I am ready to follow you. Come, Holy Spirit, and fill me with the love, power, and purposes of God. I pray these things by faith in the name of Jesus, amen.

It would be our privilege to help you get started and grow deeper in this awakened life of following Jesus. For some next steps and encouragements, visit seedbed.com/Awaken.

How the Daily Text Works

It seems obvious to say, but the Daily Text is written every day. Mostly it is written the day before it is scheduled to release online.

Before you read further, you are cordially invited to subscribe to and receive the daily e-mail. Visit seedbed.com/dailytext to get started. Also, check out the popular Facebook group, Seedbed Daily Text.

Eventually, the daily postings become part of a Daily Text discipleship resource. That's what you hold in your hands now.

It's not exactly a Bible study, though the Bible is both the source and subject. You will learn something about the Bible along the way: its history, context, original languages, and authors. The goal is not educational in nature, but transformational. Seedbed is more interested in folks knowing Jesus than knowing *about* Jesus.

To that end, each reading begins with the definitive inspiration of the Holy Spirit, the ongoing, unfolding text of Scripture. Following that is a short and, hopefully, substantive insight from the text and some aspect of its meaning. For insight to lead to deeper influence, we turn the text into prayer. Finally, influence must run its course toward impact. This is why we ask each other questions. These questions are not designed to elicit information but to crystallize intention.

Discipleship always leads from inspiration to intention and from attention to action.

Using the Daily Text as a Discipleship Curricular Resource for Groups

While Scripture always addresses us personally, it is not written to us individually. The content of Scripture cries out for a community to address. The Daily Text is made for discipleship in community. This resource can work in several different ways. It could be read like a traditional book, a few pages or chapters at a time. Though unadvisable, the readings could be crammed in on the night before the meeting. Keep in mind, the Daily Text is not called the Daily Text for kicks. We believe Scripture is worthy of our most focused and consistent attention. Every day. We all have misses, but let's make every day more than a noble aspiration. Let's make it our covenant with one another.

For Use with Bands

In our judgment, the best and highest use of the Daily Text is made through what we call banded discipleship. A band is a same-gender group of three to five people who read together, pray together, and meet together to become the love of God for one another and the world. With banded discipleship, the daily readings serve more as a common text for the band and grist for the interpersonal conversation mill between meetings. The band meeting is reserved for the specialized activities of high-bar discipleship.

To learn more about bands and banded discipleship, visit discipleshipbands.com. Be sure to download the free *Discipleship Bands: A Practical Field Guide* or order a supply of the printed booklets online. Also be sure to explore Discipleship Bands, our native app designed specifically for the practice of banded discipleship, available in the App Store or Google Play.

For Use with Classes and Small Groups

The Daily Text has also proven to be a helpful discipleship resource for a variety of small groups, from community groups to Sunday school classes. Here are some suggested guidelines for deploying the Daily Text as a resource for a small group or class setting:

1. Hearing the Text

Invite the group to settle into silence for a period of no less than one and no more than five minutes. Ask an appointed person to keep time and to read the biblical text covering the period of days since the last group meeting. Allow at least one minute of silence following the reading of the text.

2. Responding to the Text

Invite anyone from the group to respond to the reading by answering these prompts: What did you hear? What did you see? What did you otherwise sense from the Lord?

3. Sharing Insights and Implications for Discipleship

Moving in an orderly rotation (or free-for-all), invite people to share insights and implications from the week's readings.

What did you find challenging, encouraging, provocative, comforting, invasive, inspiring, corrective, affirming, guiding, or warning? Allow group conversation to proceed at will. Limit to one sharing item per turn, with multiple rounds of discussion.

4. Shaping Intentions for Prayer

Invite each person in the group to share a single discipleship intention for the week ahead. It is helpful if the intention can also be framed as a question the group can use to check in from the prior week. At each person's turn, he or she is invited to share how their intention went during the previous week. The class or group can open and close their meeting according to their established patterns.

Preface

What is the most practical question of every day of our lives?

What time is it?

As I write, it is 9:06 a.m. on Sunday, July 26, 2020.

The answer reveals my time pieces: clock and calendar.

The clock tells me what's next today. The calendar tells me what's coming next week.

The calendar tells us what is important. The clock tells us what is urgent. For most people on planet Earth, this is about where it ends. As a result, we mostly bounce back and forth like a Ping-Pong ball between the paddles of the urgent and the important. This reality, set against the backdrop of the brokenness in our own stories, accounts for 99 percent of the anxiety in our lives. Consequently, we tend to talk about time the same way we talk about money. We spend it, waste it, invest it, desperately try to manage it, and even, at times, kill it. Even more anxiety, right?

The temptation is to try to carve out a little compartment of time every day to meditate on ultimate things. It's better than nothing, but the truth is it just brings matters of ultimate concern into its own category where it must compete with everything else for the priority of one's time. What we need is a way for ultimate things to become our overarching framework and underlying foundation rather than just another compartment or category—some way of keeping the main thing the main thing all the time. But how?

So what's the main thing?

"The grass withers, the flower fades; but the word of our God will stand forever" (Isa. 40:8).

The Word of God, written down in a book we call the Bible, and incarnate in human flesh—at the right hand of God—Jesus Christ, is the main thing.

We don't keep the main thing the main thing by blocking out a few minutes every day to dedicate to reading the Bible and praying. No, we keep the main thing the main thing by making Jesus Christ Lord over all of our time; by keeping our eyes fixed on him; by taking every thought captive to him; by abiding in him second by second, minute by minute, hour by hour, day by day, week by week, month by month, year after year, until our life on earth ends and we go to him or he comes again and fully and finally establishes his kingdom on earth—whichever comes first.

This is what the Christian New Year is all about. This is why we have a Christian calendar. The Christian calendar is nothing more or less than the biblical way of translating the Word of God into our calendars and onto our clocks, which is the only way it can ever show up in real time in our everyday lives. It's why I call it the Awakening Calendar. The Awakening Calendar has one agenda: to keep us in constant touch with the glory of God the Father, through the love of Jesus Christ, in the power of the Holy Spirit—from our highest aspirations to our most practical applications. The Awakening Calendar translates the movemental life of Jesus Christ into the most practical movements of our lives and communities.

The Word of God (a.k.a. the Bible) by which we know the Word (a.k.a. Jesus) is the single most important time-telling device in the history of history and in the future of eternity. Perhaps you noticed the map-like drawing on the cover and on page ii of the book. You will note it is the life of Jesus Christ mapped out in a linear movemental fashion. It coheres around three epic journeys: the journey of Advent through Epiphany: darkness to light; the journey of Lent through Easter: death to life; and the journey of Pentecost through Kingdomtide: brokenness to wholeness.

It begins at the highest summit where we gaze upon the furthest horizon we can grasp and behold the second Advent (coming) of our Lord Jesus Christ. From there we embark on a journey of descent, narrated by prophets and leading us to a field with shepherds and angels and onward to a baby wrapped in swaddling cloths and laying in a manger— Christmas. After a twelve day celebration we enter the next leg of the journey: Epiphany. It begins always on January 6 with the telling story of the wise kings who came from the far east, who discovered the mystery not from the prophets but from the stars. From here we move on a path of ascent, through miracles, mysteries, and manifestations until we reach the summit of what history calls "The Mount of Transfiguration." It is another of the high places of the story, where we can almost reach out and touch eternity—so glorious we will want to make permanent encampment. This begins the second epic journey.

Journey two takes us into the descent of all descents as we follow Jesus through forty days of wilderness all the way down to the cross. Maundy Thursday leads to Good Friday and Holy Saturday and the surprise of all surprises: Easter Sunday and the resurrection of Jesus Christ from the dead. Here begins an ascent leading us through fifty days we call Eastertide. On the fortieth day we watch as Jesus ascends into the clouds to the right hand of God. Ten days later we gather on the day of Pentecost where he sends the promised Holy Spirit upon the gathered people of God and the church is born.

Journey three finds us filled with the Spirit on the now well-worn path of descent into the valley of vision where we follow Jesus into the kingdom of on earth as it is in heaven, doing the things he did and even greater things. From here we embark on a movement we call Kingdomtide, winding our way back up to the summit of the King of all kings where we again gaze upon the far Advent horizon to behold his coming again.

This map sketch is meant to convey the reality that time is not a neverending cyclical process but the movement of God with us. Though there be a beginning, middle, and end, this is the world without end.

There is much more to say. This is only the sketch. It is time for Advent now. It is time for the Christian New Year.

We are embarked.

Introduction

"Wake up, sleeper, rise from the dead, and Christ will shine on you."

—Ephesians 5:14 NIV

Happy New Year! It's time to sow for a great awakening!

Happy New Year? "But wait," you say, "it's not January 1." Right, but Christians have a different year. Our year begins with the first Sunday of Advent. We begin by lifting our sights to the far horizon of the last and final great awakening—the second coming of Jesus Christ. Advent is a season of great awakening. That's what this book you hold in your hands is all about. It is an invitation to awaken the dawn of a new year and, in doing so, to awaken to the grace of God in Jesus Christ like we never imagined possible. This means a deeper attachment to God, to our true selves, our families, our church, and our neighbors in our towns and cities and away to the ends of the earth. After all, we don't need more connections, we need deeper and more whole and holy attachments. The sun is rising, and the light is dawning on a new year and a new day. Might we begin by awakening the dawn of Advent?

When it comes to sunrise services, we think first of Easter morning, the dawn that brought the news of the resurrection of Jesus Christ from the dead. I remember them as a child as unwelcome interruptions coming between hunting Easter eggs and eating chocolate Easter bunnies. But I remember them; they were unforgettable. Sitting or standing in some farmer's dew-covered field just on the outskirts of town, surrounded by the local saints from the First United Methodist Church, belting out "Up from the Grave He Arose" in our best predawn voices, and hearing the news declared once again, "He is risen!" and meeting it with our annual response, "He is risen, indeed!"

We remember them. It's funny how these peculiar activities of the people of God take acts of remembering ancient things and translate them into the indelible memories of our own time. It is as though something that happened thousands of years ago mysteriously happens again. Waking up early, showing up in pre-Sunday morning best, singing in a field . . . as a kid, you don't exactly understand it at the time, yet you never forget it.

So why are we talking about Easter in Advent? For starters, it's only because of Easter that we have Advent. It's an obvious thing to say that there would be no Easter without Christmas. The corollary is less obvious, yet even more true: there would be no Christmas without Easter. If Jesus is not raised from the dead, there would be no point in having Christmas. A miraculous birth story of a Galilean peasant would fade into the sunset of history as a curious myth of no consequence.

The resurrection of Jesus Christ from the dead gives history its meaning, and it gives the future its deepest destiny.

Because of the resurrection we remember the story of his first coming to us at Christmas. And, yes, because of the resurrection, we anticipate the story of his second coming at the end of the age and the great resurrection of the dead—and the life everlasting.

Years ago I came across the story of a young Roman Catholic priest from Poland. Karol Wojtyla served in the days of fierce Communist oppression in his country. In 1949, Communist leaders built a utopian city. It was meant to demonstrate the triumph of the ideals of socialism, among them the virtues of atheism. The city was called Nowa Huta. Because they were able to engineer the city from the ground up, the law forbade the construction of churches.

From early on, the largely working-class citizens who made up the population of the city cried out for a church. In 1959, the young priest instituted a movement of holy resistance. On Christmas Eve, he led his fledgling flock to a field on the outskirts of the city where they celebrated the mass and planted a cross in the ground. The authorities promptly removed the cross the following day. Year after year the resistance gathered in the field on Christmas Eve, celebrated the mass, and planted the cross, after which it would be removed by the Communist authorities. In 1967, the city granted them a permit to build a church. After great struggle, they finally completed construction of the church, naming it "The Lord's Ark" from its likeness to Noah's ark. In 1977, the young priest who led the long holy resistance of the cross consecrated the church. The very next year, in 1978, something happened that stunned the world. This obscure Polish priest, Karol Wojtyla, was named as the pope of the Roman Catholic Church, John Paul II.

Barely a decade later, the world witnessed the incredible collapse of Communism and the fall of the Soviet Union. We trace it back to the fledgling flock of the kingdom of heaven, who mustered up the humble audacity to plant a cross in a field at midnight on Christmas Eve year after year after year.

The story electrified me. At the time, I served as dean of the chapel at Asbury Theological Seminary in a little town tucked into the rolling pastures of rural Kentucky. I gathered a small flock of seminary students for an Advent awakening service. On the first Sunday of Advent, we gathered in the chilly predawn darkness on a bluegrass field on the outskirts of town. We read Scripture, lit candles, sang songs, prayed our way into the dawn, celebrated the Eucharist, and planted a cross. Then we all went to my house and feasted on pancakes, bacon, eggs, sausage, and the fellowship of the Holy Spirit.

I've been doing it every year since, more than a decade now. The first Sunday of Advent, the beginning of the Christian year, is New Year's Day for the church. While Easter marks the massive movement from death to life, Advent marks the cosmic shift from darkness to light. What better time for a sunrise awakening service than the dawn of a new year, a new Advent?

I want to invite you into such a practice this Advent. Whether with your church, your family, a few friends, or all by yourself (which I've done before), would you be willing to interrupt the predictable pattern of past years and try something new?

Would you dare to get outside of the bounds of church as usual, look to the horizon of his coming, and declare, "*Maranatha*! Come, Lord Jesus!"

Would you look out on the fresh calendar of a new year ahead and pray, "Yet, O Lord, you are our Father; we are the clay, and you are our potter; we are all the work of your hand" (Isa. 64:8)?

Would you sing with faith into the morning sky, "O Come, O Come, Emmanuel and ransom captive Israel"?

Would you break the bread and share the cup of the body and blood of our Lord Jesus Christ?

Might you even bind a couple of boards or sticks together into a cross and plant it in the ground as an act of holy resistance to the kingdoms of this world?

Imagine churches scattered all across our land, maybe even the globe, venturing to the outskirts of towns and cities (or gathering in public parks and city squares), standing, declaring, singing, praying, eating, drinking, planting, indeed, sowing crosses into the soil of our communities.

This is the stuff of sowing for a great awakening. And I promise you, it will arrest your soul and your children will never forget it.

Happy New Year! It's time to sow for a great awakening!

THE
CHRISTIAN
NEW
YEAR

Remember the Future

REVELATION 21:1–4 NIV | Then I saw "a new heaven and a new earth," for the first heaven and the first earth had passed away, and there was no longer any sea. I saw the Holy City, the new Jerusalem, coming down out of heaven from God, prepared as a bride beautifully dressed for her husband. And I heard a loud voice from the throne saying, "Look! God's dwelling place is now among the people, and he will dwell with them. They will be his people, and God himself will be with them and be their God. 'He will wipe every tear from their eyes. There will be no more death' or mourning or crying or pain, for the old order of things has passed away."

Consider This

The word *advent* has a very simple meaning: the arrival or coming of a notable person, thing, or event. The church has an ancient saying we call "The Mystery of Faith." During the celebration of the Lord's Supper, the people speak this mystery in unison. We declare, "Christ has died. Christ is risen. Christ will come again." Most of the time, the church is pretty faithful to remember and celebrate the first two elements of this great mystery, the death and resurrection of Jesus Christ. When it comes to the third element, the second coming of Jesus, we can be a little more reticent. We believe it, but because it remains in the future, we can't exactly remember it. Or can we?

By the grace of the revelation of the Word of God, we know the whole story: from beginning to end; from creation to new creation. "Christ has died. Christ is risen. Christ will come again." For centuries, the season of Advent has created an opportunity to remember that which remains in the future. In fact, before Advent was ever about the first coming of Jesus Christ, it was about his second coming. The second coming of Jesus will mark the end of all things broken and the beginning of all things made new. It will be a glorious day, and yet we must be prepared. It is only in remembering the future second coming that we can most deeply appreciate and appropriate Christmas, his first coming.

Whether fact or fiction, stories come with three parts: beginning, middle, and end. The best stories have the longest middles, but the risk of a long middle is that we can lose sight of the end. It's not the plot that keeps us turning the pages, but the glorious hope of the end, the final resolution. The end is not our death and going to a better place, which is mere comfort. The end is a new heaven and a new earth. That is hope. In this light, I want to ask you to read the following words from the end of the story. Read them aloud, slowly, and deliberately, as though your life depends on it. Why? Because your life depends on it.

Then I saw "a new heaven and a new earth," for the first heaven and the first earth had passed away, and there was no longer any sea. I saw the Holy City, the new Jerusalem, coming down out of heaven from God, prepared as a bride beautifully dressed for her husband. And I heard a loud voice from the throne saying,

"Look! God's dwelling place is now among the people, and he will dwell with them. They will be his people, and God himself will be with them and be their God. 'He will wipe every tear from their eyes. There will be no more death' or mourning or crying or pain, for the old order of things has passed away."

With the first Advent of Jesus Christ, the story shifted from a miry middle to a new beginning—the beginning of the end. We now find ourselves awaiting his coming again when he will bring the new creation. And so we begin again, in a brand new year, with clear vision and renewed hope, somewhere in the middle of the beginning of the end.

The Prayer

Our Father in heaven, nearer than my breath, thank you for these days of Advent and this new year in Christ. You are the Alpha and the Omega, the beginning and the end. Awaken me to you afresh. I am ready to begin again—not starting over, for with you nothing is lost or wasted, but beginning again. Filled with faith, hope, and love, I will awaken now, somewhere in the middle of the beginning of the end. In the name of Jesus Messiah—the one who has come, is here, and is coming again—for his glory and our good. Amen.

The Questions

- What might a new year, a new beginning, a fresh start look like for you on this first day of December? How will you mark this time—neither with idealism or realism but with faith, hope, and love?

2 Learning to Stand on a Word

LUKE 21:25–36 | "There will be signs in the sun, the moon, and the stars, and on the earth distress among nations confused by the roaring of the sea and the waves. People will faint from fear and foreboding of what is coming upon the world, for the powers of the heavens will be shaken. Then they will see 'the Son of Man coming in a cloud' with power and great glory. Now when these things begin to take place, stand up and raise your heads, because your redemption is drawing near."

Then he told them a parable: "Look at the fig tree and all the trees; as soon as they sprout leaves you can see for yourselves and know that summer is already near. So also, when you see these things taking place, you know that the kingdom of God is near. Truly I tell you, this generation will not pass away until all things have taken place. Heaven and earth will pass away, but my words will not pass away.

"Be on guard so that your hearts are not weighed down with dissipation and drunkenness and the worries of this life, and that day does not catch you unexpectedly, like a trap. For it will come upon all who live on the face of the whole earth. Be alert at all times, praying that you may have the strength to escape all these things that will take place, and to stand before the Son of Man."

Consider This

The words of Jesus, though clear, were often filled with mystery—not so much when he said this:

"Heaven and earth will pass away, but my words will not pass away."

Advent offers a marvelous opportunity for awakening to his words in a deeper way; indeed, to awaken to the whole counsel of the Word of God. How might we engage the Scriptures more intentionally in these days of Advent? Try reading each day's Scripture text aloud, so you can hear it with your ears. Perhaps share readings around the family dinner table. Select particular texts to meditate and ruminate over. Choose a verse, like this one, to write on an index card and commit to memory:

"Heaven and earth will pass away, but my words will not pass away."

I am forever indebted to Mrs. Betty Jane, a woman of God from my hometown growing up. It never failed. Every time I visited the small Main Street furniture store, the aging widow asked me the question, "John David, what word are you standing on today?" It brings to mind the old standard hymn, "Standing on the promises of Christ the Lord, bound to Him eternally by love's strong cord, overcoming daily with the Spirit's sword, standing on the promises of God."* Mrs. Betty Jane always knew the Word on which she stood. It's

---

* Russell Kelso Carter, "Standing on the Promises of Christ My King," 1886. Public domain.

where I first learned this word from the prophet Isaiah: "The grass withers and the flowers fall, but the word of our God endures forever" (Isa. 40:8 NIV). Over the years it's become a well-grooved word in my soul. For on that day when he comes, the Word will be the only place left to stand. And what a spacious, beautiful place it will be.

Today's text tells the truth of this prophecy of Isaiah, of withering grass and fading flowers. They point us to the end. The signs seem distressing and even fearful:

"People will faint from fear and foreboding of what is coming upon the world, for the powers of the heavens will be shaken."

Should we be afraid? No, says the Lord, only prepared. It will not be a time of fainting in fear, but of standing in faith. Speaking of the end of all things broken and the beginning of all things new, Clive Staples Lewis, writing in the middle of the last century, put it ever so eloquently, if not electrifying:

> When the author walks on to the stage the play is over. God is going to invade, all right: but what is the good of saying you are on His side then, when you see the whole natural universe melting away like a dream and something else—something it never entered your head to conceive—comes crashing in; something so beautiful to some of us and so terrible to others that none of us will have any choice left? For this time it will be God without disguise; something so overwhelming that it will strike either irresistible love or irresistible horror into every creature. It will be too late then to choose your side. There is no use saying you choose

to lie down when it has become impossible to stand up. That will not be the time for choosing; it will be the time when we discover which side we really have chosen, whether we realised it before or not. Now, today, this moment, is our chance to choose the right side. God is holding back to give us that chance. It will not last for ever. We must take it or leave it.[*]

The Prayer

Our Father in heaven, nearer than my breath, thank you for these days of Advent and this new year in Christ. I confess the thought of your second coming both frightens and comforts me. Root out the fear from my life as so many weeds growing there, sucking up the water, the nutrients, and the energy from the soil of my heart. I want to sow the seeds of faith into the seedbed of my mind. Let this Advent become an extravagant sowing of faith. Come, Holy Spirit, and water those seeds. In the name of Jesus Messiah—the one who has come, is here, and is coming again—for his glory and our good, amen.

The Questions

· Does the second coming of Jesus Christ scare you or stir you? How might you participate in the work of the Spirit to root out the weeds of fear and sow the seeds of faith? How will you engage the Word of God in fresh ways in this new year?

---

[*] C. S. Lewis, *Mere Christianity* (New York: HarperCollins, 2011), 65.

3 Asking the Deeper Questions

ISAIAH 2:1–5 | The word that Isaiah son of Amoz saw concerning Judah and Jerusalem.

In days to come
   the mountain of the LORD's house
shall be established as the highest of the mountains,
   and shall be raised above the hills;
all the nations shall stream to it.
   Many peoples shall come and say,
"Come, let us go up to the mountain of the LORD,
   to the house of the God of Jacob;
that he may teach us his ways
   and that we may walk in his paths."
For out of Zion shall go forth instruction,
   and the word of the LORD from Jerusalem.
He shall judge between the nations,
   and shall arbitrate for many peoples;
they shall beat their swords into plowshares,
   and their spears into pruning hooks;
nation shall not lift up sword against nation,
   neither shall they learn war any more.

O house of Jacob,
   come, let us walk
   in the light of the LORD!

Consider This

Can you even imagine it?

Nation shall not lift up sword against nation, neither shall they learn war any more.

So stuck we are in the status quo of chaos and conflict that we can hardly fathom a future without it. This is the news of the day, every day, every month, every year—shots fired; soldiers dead. We invent acronyms like IEDs to efficiently say things like "improvised explosive devices," which mean roadside bombs. They explode in crowded markets and on otherwise peaceful roads going to the wrong places and kill hundreds of people at a time, while permanently trauma-tizing the brains and minds of everyone within the blast zone. And all of this so someone can be king of another hill.

We accept it as the new normal. "It's just the world we live in," we tell ourselves. All the while the ancient oracles never stop crying out:

Nation shall not lift up sword against nation, neither shall they learn war any more.

Far from a utopian vision of the socially engineered peace of political correctness, the Bible gives us real prophets, but they are not realists. Neither are they optimists. They are what I call hopefulists. They do not deny the reality of swords and spears. They reveal a deeper destiny:

They shall beat their swords into plowshares, and their spears into pruning hooks.

They see weapons taken out of the military industrial complex and the business of fear and returned to the service of farming.

It's time to ask these questions: What of my life? Am I fashioning myself as a sword or being fashioned into a plow? I want to be sharpened for the glory of God; but I must be bent instead for the glory of the ground. I want to climb the mountain, take the hill, ascend to greatness; but I must learn to churn the soil so my children might come after me sowing seeds of light. What will be my legacy? What do I leave in my wake—a fertile furrow or a monument to myself?

They shall beat their swords into plowshares, and their spears into pruning hooks.

These words are not practical, you say. And you are correct. These words purpose to unshackle us from the false security of a safe existence. You were made for more. You were made for glory. You were crafted to express the impractical extravagance of holy love. Can you even imagine it?

The Prayer

Our Father in heaven, nearer than my breath, thank you for these days of Advent and this new year in Christ. Thank you for your vision that has never wavered. From those first warring brothers of Cain and Abel to the warring nations of our time, you have never wavered from your vision of perfect peace. Forgive me for my cynical realism that scoffs at biblical idealism. I will stop. There is no such thing as biblical idealism, only truth. Swords into plows. Yes, Lord. I don't see it yet, but yes, I will believe. Come, Holy Spirit, and translate this truth into my small life that I might grow larger in the Lord. In the name of Jesus Messiah—the one who has come, is here, and is coming again—for his glory and our good, amen.

The Questions

- Do you tend to write off such language as hopeful idealism and dismiss it? What will it take for your mind to bend into the shape of God's Word—from a sword into a plow?

Why Cynicism Is Soul Cancer and the Cure

4

ISAIAH 11:1–10 NIV | A shoot will come up from the stump of Jesse; from his roots a Branch will bear fruit.
    The Spirit of the Lord will rest on him—
      the Spirit of wisdom and of understanding,
      the Spirit of counsel and of might,
      the Spirit of the knowledge and fear of the Lord—
    and he will delight in the fear of the Lord.

He will not judge by what he sees with his eyes,
    or decide by what he hears with his ears;
but with righteousness he will judge the needy,
    with justice he will give decisions for the poor of the earth.
He will strike the earth with the rod of his mouth;
    with the breath of his lips he will slay the wicked.
Righteousness will be his belt
    and faithfulness the sash around his waist.

The wolf will live with the lamb,
  the leopard will lie down with the goat,
the calf and the lion and the yearling together;
  and a little child will lead them.
The cow will feed with the bear,
  their young will lie down together,
  and the lion will eat straw like the ox.
The infant will play near the cobra's den,
  and the young child will put its hand into the viper's nest.
They will neither harm nor destroy
  on all my holy mountain,
for the earth will be filled with the knowledge of the LORD
  as the waters cover the sea.

In that day the Root of Jesse will stand as a banner for the peoples; the nations will rally to him, and his resting place will be glorious.

Consider This

For the earth will be filled with the knowledge of the LORD as the waters cover the sea.

Wow! Just wow! It's time to train our eyes to see the beatific vision, to hone our sight on the horizon, to learn to behold the *glorious state of the future.* In order to do this, we must rid ourselves of the soul's cancer: cynicism. The cynic cloaks himself in the wise disguise of a realist. Truth be told, realism is just another name for a defeated idealism. Cynicism is the bitter fruit of a desecrated imagination. Cynicism treats the sickness of our hopelessness with the topical ointment of our thinly veiled anger.

Newsflash: the Bible is not a book of idealism but of realism. Here's the vision of biblical realism:

The wolf will live with the lamb, the leopard will lie down with the goat, the calf and the lion and the yearling together; and a little child will lead them. The cow will feed with the bear, their young will lie down together, and the lion will eat straw like the ox.

The Holy Spirit longs to fill and feed our anemic imaginations with such vision. Will we let him? It starts with dwelling on such words. No time like Advent to begin.

So why do we rush to those angry, armchair, dime-store prophets who can only assuage our fears by blaming the Republicans or the Democrats? Advent calls saying, "Listen to these prophets of the arduous and adjacent possible. Let them encompass your weary imagination. They offer no easy solutions. They impart vision. We perish without it." That's what cynicism is: dead people who still have a pulse. But remember, a pulse means there's still a possibility.

It's time that we come to terms with this fact: the return of the Lord is a good thing. Is it not? But, you say, there are so many people I know who are not ready for this—the end of all things broken and the fulfillment of all things made new. And so, the Advent New Year's question of questions: What about these people you love? Have you spoken to them concerning the end of all things broken and the fulfillment of all things made new? And how about you? Are you ready? If not, there is only one good reason.

It is because you are not sure the return of the Lord is a good thing.

Think about it. The return of the Lord means no more child slavery. No more sex trade. No more cancer. No more drug addiction. No more tears. No more terrorism. No more war. No more starvation. No more wheelchairs. The sheen of newness everywhere. The contagion of gladness spreading, filling the earth "as the waters cover the sea."

The Prayer

Our Father in heaven, nearer than my breath, thank you for these days of Advent and this new year in Christ. You will indeed fill the earth with the knowledge of the Lord as the waters cover the sea. I confess my cynical outlook; I have allowed the low-bar discourse of this world and its news to lower the tide of your good news in my soul. Open my mind and heart to more of your Word, to more of you. Come, Holy Spirit, wake me up, and make all of this fiercely practical in these days of Advent. In the name of Jesus Messiah—the one who has come, is here, and is coming again—for his glory and our good, amen.

The Question

- Spend the next five minutes simply reading and ruminating over the biblical text for today. It is medicine for your soul. Only the therapy of Word and Spirit can cure the soul's cancer of cynicism. How deep do the roots of cynicism go into your soul?

Sing the New Old Song

5

ZEPHANIAH 3:14–20 | Sing aloud, O daughter Zion;
shout, O Israel!
Rejoice and exult with all your heart,
O daughter Jerusalem!
The LORD has taken away the judgments against you,
he has turned away your enemies.
The king of Israel, the LORD, is in your midst;
you shall fear disaster no more.
On that day it shall be said to Jerusalem:
Do not fear, O Zion;
do not let your hands grow weak.
The LORD, your God, is in your midst,
a warrior who gives victory;
he will rejoice over you with gladness,
he will renew you in his love;
he will exult over you with loud singing
as on a day of festival.
I will remove disaster from you,
so that you will not bear reproach for it.
I will deal with all your oppressors
at that time.
And I will save the lame
and gather the outcast,

and I will change their shame into praise
  and renown in all the earth.
At that time I will bring you home,
  at the time when I gather you;
for I will make you renowned and praised
  among all the peoples of the earth,
when I restore your fortunes
  before your eyes, says the LORD.

Consider This

He will exult over you with loud singing as on a day of festival.

Have you ever wondered what he is singing? I want it to be something like, "We Are the Champions" or, "The Eye of the Tiger," or some epically triumphant theme song from a movie yet to be made. What does he sing over me? In this new year, might it be time for a new song, or at least an old song made new?

At the epicenter of all that exists, a song is playing. Can you hear it? At the heart of the Bible, literally in the middle of the book, is a short book called the Song of Songs. Isn't that something? In the middle of sixty-six books we get a song, and it's not just any song. It's the song of all songs. At the core of this song of all songs is a simple chorus of five words. It is the glad song of the Beloved. It is the exultant song of the Bridegroom. It is the expectant song of the future. It is the theme song of the Warrior God of Peace. It has only five primal Hebrew words: "My Beloved Mine; I His."

This is the song of the Holy Spirit, the song of the Father to the Son as the whole of creation was breathed into being by the breath of his Word. This is the song of the Son to the Father as his broken body breathed his last breath of love. This is the song of the Bride back to the Bridegroom as the skies will one day roll back like a scroll: "My Beloved Mine; I His." It is the soundtrack of the future that plays in the present for all with ears to hear. Noted missiologist Peter Kuzmich once said, "Hope is the ability to hear the music of the future. Faith is having the courage to dance to that song today."

This song of all songs—My Beloved Mine; I His—brings the whole picture into crystal-clear focus. The core of the core message of the gospel of God, the message on every page of Scripture, can be brought down to a single term: bonded attachment. The central and really only commandment of God is to love God, love others, and love ourselves (see Matthew 22:36–40). It naturally follows: the true meaning of life is found in bonded attachments to God, others, and self. It begins, middles, and ends in our progressive ability to believe, hear, and sing along in this song of our own belovedness: "My Beloved Mine; I His."

For the first five hundred years of the church, this tiny allegorical book, the Song of Songs, was all the theologians wanted to talk about. So much more than a description of marital passion, the Song of Songs is a mysterious analogy of the love of Father, Son, and Holy Spirit. They were enthralled with the bonded attachments of Father, Son, and Holy Spirit and how we, the image-bearers of God, were made for these same bonded attachments with God, others, and ourselves. Some years ago I found myself dwelling deep in the mystery of this text. As I was ruminating on these five words, a simple melody emerged. I shared the melody with a songwriter, worship leader, friend of mine. He added a powerful chorus, a bold choir, and recorded it. It's a little-known song by a well-known singer, and I would like you to hear it today. Google "My Beloved" by Chris Tomlin, and you will find it.

He will exult over you with loud singing as on a day of festival.

The Prayer

Our Father in heaven, nearer than my breath, thank you for these days of Advent and this new year in Christ. You will indeed fill the earth with the knowledge of the Lord as the waters cover the sea. I confess my cynical outlook; I have allowed the low-bar discourse of this world and its news to lower the tide of your good news in my soul. Open my mind and heart to more of your Word, to more of you. Come, Holy Spirit, wake me up, and make all of this fiercely practical in these days of Advent. In the name of Jesus Messiah—the one who has come, is here, and is coming again—for his glory and our good, amen.

The Questions

- Where do you think your weakest sense of bonded attachment is in your life? With God? Others? Self? Why do you think this is so?

Finding a Higher Calendar

6

2 PETER 3:8–15 NIV | But do not forget this one thing, dear friends: With the Lord a day is like a thousand years, and a thousand years are like a day. The Lord is not slow in keeping his promise, as some understand slowness. Instead he is patient with you, not wanting anyone to perish, but everyone to come to repentance.

But the day of the Lord will come like a thief. The heavens will disappear with a roar; the elements will be destroyed by fire, and the earth and everything done in it will be laid bare.

Since everything will be destroyed in this way, what kind of people ought you to be? You ought to live holy and godly lives as you look forward to the day of God and speed its coming. That day will bring about the destruction of the heavens by fire, and the elements will melt in the heat. But in keeping with his promise we are looking forward to a new heaven and a new earth, where righteousness dwells.

So then, dear friends, since you are looking forward to this, make every effort to be found spotless, blameless and at peace with him. Bear in mind that our Lord's patience means salvation, just as our dear brother Paul also wrote you with the wisdom that God gave him.

Consider This

With the Lord a day is like a thousand years, and a thousand years are like a day.

Can we agree that the Lord works off of a higher calendar? This is why it is so important for us to mark time with a much larger memory than the events of our times. We are part of a much larger story than that of family, country, or even this world. Our story spans from eternity past through all of history and onward through eternity future. It's why the followers of Jesus need a bigger calendar than the Roman calendar. While January through December aren't going anywhere, we need our calendars to be infused with the story of Jesus and the timing of God.

In America, we live in a country marked by a couple of centuries. The Israelites spent four hundred years in Egypt alone before the hand of God delivered them from the land of slavery into the land of promise. Between the last Word of God to Malachi and the first New Testament Word of God to Zechariah, we count four hundred years of silence. Two hundred years are a mere watch in the night on the Lord's calendar.

To say this tests the patience of the average person would be an understatement. We read. We believe. We hope. But it's been more than two thousand years since he came the first time—730,000 days! Come on, Jesus! We are ready for the new heaven and the new earth. We are ready for no more suffering, the end of injustice, no more children sold into slavery or the sex trade, no more cancer, no more divorce, no more war. We are ready, Jesus. Aren't you looking forward to this? Two thousand years now, the vigil passed from generation to generation.

But we will keep perspective in our patience, for according to the Lord's calendar, it's only been a couple of days.

The Lord is not slow in keeping his promise, as some understand slowness. Instead he is patient with you, not wanting anyone to perish, but everyone to come to repentance.

According to the text, we misunderstand slowness. Because we know ourselves, we tend to think of slowness as procrastination. There is a difference between procrastination and patience. Our God does not delay. He waits, and he does not wait passively but actively. The Holy Spirit is at work in every single person in the world, actively calling, beckoning, wooing them to follow Jesus Christ. He patiently waits on everyone, anyone, anywhere at any time to respond with faith.

He wants this same kind of patient, active waiting for us. While we look toward the first Advent and wait on the final one, we actively move about our days and lives with confidence that the Spirit is moving in every single person we encounter to bring them into relationship and an ever-deepening walk with Jesus. Jesus would reach out to them through us, perhaps with a smile, an embrace, a surprising act of mercy, a word of grace or mercy, even an explicit sharing of the gospel as he leads.

Bear in mind that our Lord's patience means salvation.

It is a brand-new year. Can we get on the same page on Jesus' calendar? It's Advent, a season where the air is pregnant with the Holy Spirit's awakening power.

The Prayer

Our Father in heaven, nearer than my breath, thank you for these days of Advent and this new year in Christ. I confess

I have lost touch and maybe even patience with the expansive scope of your calendar and timing. Wake me up to the possibility that you could return today. Turn my waiting from passive to active. Come, Holy Spirit, and attune my spirit to your working in every person I will encounter today. In the name of Jesus Messiah—the one who has come, is here, and is coming again—for his glory and our good, amen.

The Questions

- How might you become more attuned and alert to the fact that God is at work in every single person on the face of the earth, especially the ones you will encounter today? What could that look like?

7 Assessing Our Snooze-Bar Habits

ROMANS 13:11–14 | Besides this, you know what time it is, how it is now the moment for you to wake from sleep. For salvation is nearer to us now than when we became believers; the night is far gone, the day is near. Let us then lay aside the works of darkness and put on the armor of light; let us live honorably as in the day, not in reveling and drunkenness, not in debauchery and licentiousness, not in quarreling and jealousy. Instead, put on the Lord Jesus Christ, and make no provision for the flesh, to gratify its desires.

Consider This

The New Testament of the Bible is a marvel in so many ways. Those earliest, most immediate followers of Jesus—witnesses to his life, words, signs, deeds, miraculous works, suffering, death, resurrection, and ascension—wrote it all down. They were in the room on the day of Pentecost when the Holy Spirit fell upon those awestruck apostles. From this greatest of all awakenings, the gospel rode on the wings of the wind of the Spirit into the streets of the city of Jerusalem and onward into all Judea and outward into Samaria and away to the ends of the earth.

Over two millennia later, this awakening message keeps on going, pursuing every heart, knocking on the door of every home, hovering with possibility over every church, compassing the perimeter of every city, leaving no stone unturned. At this point in history, twenty-one centuries later, billions of awakening stories cry out in the wake of the awakening movement of the gospel of Jesus Christ.

Yes, the New Testament of the Bible is a marvel, but from the very earliest days, before being bound in books called Bibles, before the ink could dry on the scrolls, we already see a stunning surprise: sleep. The awakened are slipping back into the slumber of sleep. Only thirteen chapters into the first letter in our Bibles, the one we call Romans, an alarm clock goes off:

Besides this, you know what time it is, how it is now the moment for you to wake from sleep. For salvation is nearer to us now than when we became believers.

Do you remember when you first became a believer? Perhaps this awakening is afoot for the first time in your life now? Either way, if those earliest followers of Jesus could drift off to sleep at the wheel, couldn't it happen to you? It's not that we stop believing; we just drift off to sleep. Our belief becomes brittle. All the shiny new things ever about us and the subtle seduction of darkness can be almost overwhelming.

Let us then lay aside the works of darkness and put on the armor of light; let us live honorably as in the day, not in reveling and drunkenness, not in debauchery and licentiousness, not in quarreling and jealousy.

These days leading up to Christmas have a way of bringing brokenness to the surface. The buzz of another glass of bourbon and bottle of wine have a way of pushing it back beneath our awareness. Every day the world makes more and more provision for the flesh, more places to hide from the light. What if we took a different approach? What might it mean to stop fighting the darkness and instead simply "put on the armor of light"? The light hurts our eyes at first, but its gift is to give us vision.

Jesus stands at the door of Advent knocking, not to ruin Christmas parties but to bring the deeper celebrations we were made for. What would it look like to "put on the Lord Jesus Christ" in these days of Advent? It is as simple as opening the door and inviting him in. "I am the light of the world," he said, "whoever follows me will never walk in darkness but will have the light of life" (John 8:12). You can't beat the darkness. He already has. Be it the first time or the thousandth, here are the words he's waiting to hear from the voice of your deepest heart: "Come in, Jesus."

The Prayer

Our Father in heaven, nearer than my breath, thank you for these days of Advent and this new year in Christ. Make them be for me days of awakening—to your good-ness, to your better-ness, to your best-ness. Wrap me in the armor of light. Come, Holy Spirit, wrap me in the arms of the life and love of Jesus and make me such a person of embrace for others. In the name of Jesus Messiah—the one who has come, is here, and is coming again—for his glory and our good, amen.

The Questions

· On a scale of 1 to 10 (10 being the highest), how would you assess the sleepiness of your soul? Do you have a snooze-bar habit? Are you in hibernation mode? There is no shame in the honesty game, so be honest.

Break Up Your Fallow Ground

8

HOSEA 10:12 | Sow for yourselves righteousness;
reap steadfast love;
break up your fallow ground;
for it is the time to seek the LORD,
that he may come and rain righteousness upon you.

Consider This

There's a word for soil that will not grow anything. We call it hardpan. Something happens underneath the surface when ground is not worked for a series of growing seasons. Layers of clay calcify into an impervious shield, preventing water from reaching the subsoil and stopping the possibility of any moisture from seeping back up. The result? No more topsoil to grow anything new. What once was fertile loam becomes something akin to impenetrable concrete.

Hardpan. It's an apt description for the condition of people who have lost touch with their inner life. At times, this comes from years of consistent neglect. At other times, it can be traced to a crushing event or broken relationship somewhere in the past that is still unresolved. Though it's not a foolproof test and by no means scientific, here's a telling question: When was the last time you cried?

I remember a particular day on the farm growing up. It was a day between seasons—a day between winter's resting and spring's testing. I stood by my father at the break of dawn, in a frost-caked field of fallow ground. This ground needed a deeper healing. He hooked the tractor to an implement called the subsoiler. It was a different kind of plow with long, slowly curving, ground-grabbing, claw-like tines of wrought iron steel. Though simple in its spartan design, the subsoiler required our largest tractor to pull it. As plumes of the blackest smoke rose from the tractor, the plows dug into the ground to what seemed like the depth of a grave. Reaching the stuff of the subsoil, somewhere between molten clay and petrified ash, the plow pierced to depths long deprived of the sky's breath. Unfurling ribbons of earth above the ground, the thrilling scene indelibly impacted the spirit of my childhood. As I remember it again, I feel the wondrous churn of that boyish soil rising from the subterranean depths of my fallow heart.

Might it be time for some subsoiling in your life?

The Prayer

Our Father in heaven, nearer than my breath, thank you for these days of Advent and this new year in Christ. Show me to the fallow ground in my own heart—places long neglected, even forgotten. Break through the hardpan surface with the plow of your cross. My soul must breathe the deeper air of your Spirit. So much of the past, the subsoil of my life, needs healing. Turn the soil in ways that transform my life. Come, Holy Spirit, awaken me to the possibilities that I might be willing to embrace the promise and pain of deep transformation. In the name of Jesus Messiah—the one who came, is here, and is coming again—for his glory and our good, amen.

The Questions

- Take a tour through the fields of the farm of your heart and mind. Where is the fallow ground? Will you invite the Lord to plow there with the subsoiler of his Spirit?

9 The Quiet Game

LUKE 1:68–79 | "Blessed be the Lord God of Israel,
for he has looked favorably on his people and redeemed them.
He has raised up a mighty savior for us
in the house of his servant David,
as he spoke through the mouth of his holy prophets from of old,
that we would be saved from our enemies and from the hand
of all who hate us.
Thus he has shown the mercy promised to our ancestors,
and has remembered his holy covenant,
the oath that he swore to our ancestor Abraham,
to grant us that we, being rescued from the hands of our
enemies,
might serve him without fear, in holiness and righteousness
before him all our days.
And you, child, will be called the prophet of the Most High;
for you will go before the Lord to prepare his ways,
to give knowledge of salvation to his people
by the forgiveness of their sins.
By the tender mercy of our God,
the dawn from on high will break upon us,
to give light to those who sit in darkness and in the shadow of
death, to guide our feet into the way of peace."

Consider This

Just nine months prior, the angelic being named Gabriel, who stands in the presence of God, visited Zechariah in the temple. He brought news that he and his aging wife would bear a child. Zechariah did not believe, and he was struck silent by the angel.

Fast forward to the scene of today's text. Can you picture him? There's Zechariah, the man whose tongue the angel silenced. He's holding a sign. It says in big letters, "His name is John." With Zechariah's speech now suddenly restored, the Spirit of God shatters the four hundred years of silence with this prophecy of promise, some of the most cherished words in the history of the world.

What is it about silence? It is different than mere quiet. A room can be completely silent yet still devoid of quiet. How? Because the real noise is not from without but within. Silence is the outer reality of a space without sound. Quiet is the inner reality of a heart without noise. Silence is not a prerequisite for quiet. The psalmist says, "But I have calmed and quieted myself, I am like a weaned child with its mother; like a weaned child I am content" (Ps. 131:2). Even in the midst of the noisiest surroundings, the Holy Spirit can bring us into a deep inner quiet. What a good word for a new year of faith.

As you find yourself in the silence of an early morning or late night, perhaps sitting near the glow of a Christmas tree, speak these words until they shift you from the outer silence into an inner quiet, "But I have calmed and quieted myself, I am like a weaned child with its mother; like a weaned child I am content."

Zechariah was forced into a fast from speech for a long season, because he did not have ears to hear. I suspect he learned a deeper quiet in those days, one that trained his ability to hear words and his heart to believe them. It's why we must read Scripture aloud, so our ears can hear the primal sounds of faith.

Sometimes it takes fasting from our words in order to recover their power and meaning. God intends a deepest connection between the words from his mouth and the words from our mouths. When every space is filled with our words, there is little room left for the hearing of God's words. Would you try an Advent experiment? Let's call it "The New Quiet Game." Start measuring how long you can go without speaking a word. Use the stopwatch feature on your phone with its lap timer, each lap beginning when you speak again. Like holding your breath stretches your lung capacity, see if holding your words might stretch your capacity for quiet. It will take time and attention, but it will shift things in your deeper disposition. It could have the effect of moving the furniture around in your soul. Who knows? In this kind of quiet, you could awaken to the voice of God in a whole new way. What could be better than that?

I want you to read this next word from Scripture aloud:

"By the tender mercy of our God,
the dawn from on high will break upon us,
to give light to those who sit in darkness and in the shadow
of death, to guide our feet into the way of peace."

Did you hear it? "The dawn from on high will break upon us." Doesn't dawn break from below with the rising of the sun? How does dawn break from on high? This is awakening. This is Advent.

The Prayer

Our Father in heaven, nearer than my breath, thank you for these days of Advent and this new year in Christ. I want to ponder this difference between mere outer silence and deep inward quiet. My soul is stirred, and I sense it will be stirred deeper still if I can walk in this kind of fast. Come, Holy Spirit, and quiet my spirit so I might lean into more of your words, fasting from my words. I want to awaken to your Word as never before. In the name of Jesus Messiah—the one who came, is here, and is coming again—for his glory and our good, amen.

The Questions

• Will you play "The New Quiet Game" today? How long do you think you can go today without speaking a word? Come back tomorrow and record your best (longest) "quiet" lap. Get out your phone. Turn on the stopwatch. Ready. Set. Go!

10 Listen for a Word beyond the Voices of Our Time

LUKE 3:1–6 | In the fifteenth year of the reign of Emperor Tiberius, when Pontius Pilate was governor of Judea, and Herod was ruler of Galilee, and his brother Philip ruler of the region of Ituraea and Trachonitis, and Lysanias ruler of Abilene, during the high priesthood of Annas and Caiaphas, the word of God came to John son of Zechariah in the wilderness. He went into all the region around the Jordan, proclaiming a baptism of repentance for the forgiveness of sins, as it is written in the book of the words of the prophet Isaiah,

"The voice of one crying out in the wilderness:
'Prepare the way of the LORD,
    make his paths straight.
Every valley shall be filled,
    and every mountain and hill shall be made low,
and the crooked shall be made straight,
    and the rough ways made smooth;
and all flesh shall see the salvation of God.'"

Consider This

The emperor of the mighty Roman Empire . . . the governor of the conquered country . . . the rulers of the regions . . . the high priests of Jerusalem . . . John. One of these things is not like the others. But note, the word of God did not come to the powerful elite in their palatial wealth. The word of God came to John, the prophet son of a priest, in the trackless wild.

John the Baptist gets a lot more than honorable mention in the days of Advent. This locust-eating, grizzly bear of a man does not conjure up images of chestnuts roasting over an open fire. Out of nowhere comes this towering figure who people can only describe by saying names like Elijah and Isaiah.

He is announcing a baptism of repentance. And *repentance* isn't exactly a word we associate with Christmas, but remember, it's not Christmas yet.

And what, you ask, is a baptism of repentance? Repentance means the realignment of one's life with what matters most. It's a breaking away from, a preparing for, and a running toward. It's the recognition of the mounting holy discontent in the pit of your soul. It's the awakening of anticipation, the storm before the calm.

Who hears John the Baptist today? Only the same people who heard him back then and in every age in between: people who are listening for a word beyond the voices of their own time. It's why the Word of God is so vitally important. All the voices we hear are bound either by our own day and time or the day and time in which they lived. Only the Word of God, which transcends time and space, can carry "the voice of one crying out in the wilderness: 'Prepare the way of the LORD, make his paths straight.'"

I remember the year the Mennonites showed up at our farm. They were different from any people I had ever seen or known, in a good way. They walked to the beat of a different drummer. Why did they come to our farm? They leveled land. They had the finest fleet of John Deere tractors and dirt buckets in the region. They kept them spit-shined too. Gentle, humble, and radiating stability, the Mennonites struck me as a people who were living by a Word beyond the voice of our time. The first thing they would do when they bought a new tractor was remove the radio. It is kind of ironic, though, that this community—who lived out a lifestyle of joy-filled repentance—leveled land.

"'Every valley shall be filled,
    and every mountain and hill shall be made low,
and the crooked shall be made straight,
    and the rough ways made smooth;
and all flesh shall see the salvation of God.'"

As they leveled land, they leveled life; as they leveled life, the Spirit of God leavened the world around them.

The Prayer

Our Father in heaven, nearer than my breath, thank you for these days of Advent and this new year in Christ. Thank you for the land-leveling and heart-leveling work of your Word and Spirit. Thank you for the peculiarity of John and his fearlessness to call us to repent. Come, Holy Spirit, and particularize this call to repentance in my own life. I sense it will open the way for awakening. Speak into the growing silence of my heart. I am willing. In the name of Jesus Messiah—the one who came, is here, and is coming again—for his glory and our good, amen.

The Questions

- How is the Word of God coming to you in these days of Advent? What is the shape of the wilderness you find yourself in? How is the silence coming? What's your record so far?

Count Your Coats

11

LUKE 3:7–18 | John said to the crowds that came out to be baptized by him, "You brood of vipers! Who warned you to flee from the wrath to come? Bear fruits worthy of repentance. Do not begin to say to yourselves, 'We have Abraham as our ancestor'; for I tell you, God is able from these stones to raise up children to Abraham. Even now the ax is lying at the root of the trees; every tree therefore that does not bear good fruit is cut down and thrown into the fire."

And the crowds asked him, "What then should we do?" In reply he said to them, "Whoever has two coats must share with anyone who has none; and whoever has food must do likewise." Even tax collectors came to be baptized, and they asked him, "Teacher, what should we do?" He said to them, "Collect no more than the amount prescribed for you." Soldiers also asked him, "And we, what should we do?" He said to them, "Do not extort money from anyone by threats or false accusation, and be satisfied with your wages."

As the people were filled with expectation, and all were questioning in their hearts concerning John, whether he might be the Messiah, John answered all of them by saying, "I baptize you with water; but one who is more powerful than I is coming; I am not worthy to untie the thong of his sandals. He will baptize you with the Holy Spirit and fire. His winnowing fork is in his hand, to clear his threshing floor and to gather the wheat into his granary; but the chaff he will burn with unquenchable fire."

So, with many other exhortations, he proclaimed the good news to the people.

Consider This

Two coats. It's quite the call to repentance. I like coats. I must have a dozen coats, one for every possible climate I might face. There's that Banana Republic warm-up coat, and the Barbour all-weather coat, and the Diesel pull-over coat, and the J. Crew barn coat, and the camo Mossy Oak hunting coat, and the L. L. Bean denim coat and . . . you get the picture. I like them all so much that when it comes time to give a coat away, I'll go into the way, way back of the closet and pull out an old one I don't wear anymore.

This year I'm finally going to do it. I'm going to take one of the coats I like, maybe even one of the new ones, and give it away to someone who doesn't have a coat. It's too bad John didn't tell me how many to give away if I had twelve coats.

And you? Have you counted your coats lately? We so often think of repentance as an inner feeling of sorrow over bad behavior and a resolve not to do it again. John says it's a lot bigger than this. When there are people without coats, and I have twelve . . . you get the point. Count those coats.

But wait . . . the greatest prophet who ever lived said to "bear fruits worthy of repentance." Fruits worthy of repentance—it is a fascinating concept. Fruit comes at the end of a process, not the beginning. Maybe checking the box of a donated coat isn't the ticket. Fruit begins with breaking up fallow ground, and sowing, and cultivating, and watering, and more cultivating, and waiting, and finally by God's grace, fruit. Maybe repentance can't be reduced to a transaction at Goodwill. Maybe repentance takes sustained attention and effort. By the power of his Word and Spirit, Jesus wants to reach deeper than mere behavior and into our dispositions, desires, and affections.

So, here's the invitation. Since we are now into Advent, which is the Christian's New Year, let's ask God to identify not a resolution but a New Year's repentance in our lives. Just one. It might be a symptom of something deeper, like twelve coats or a short temper or uncontrollable comfort eating or too much wine. Let's delve beneath the surface of the behavior and ask the deeper questions about the brokenness beneath. Rather than battling the behavior, what if we sowed some new seeds into our souls—seeds that could grow into very different patterns? How might we water and cultivate this new planting of the Lord in our lives? What if we focused on this one repentance until this time next year? Might we then bear fruits worthy of repentance? I bet so.

The Prayer

Our Father in heaven, nearer than my breath, thank you for these days of Advent and this new year in Christ. Thank you for calling for more than behavior management. You offer the deep change. Break up my fallow ground and show me the new seeds to sow there. Come, Holy Spirit, and tend the garden of my heart until I bear fruit worthy of repentance. In the name of Jesus Messiah—the one who came, is here, and is coming again—for his glory and our good, amen.

The Question

- What might the Lord be identifying in your life as the singular area of repentance for the next year? Think of the progress the Spirit might make in our lives through taking a longer view and going a slower pace.

12 A Better Vision for Repentance

PHILIPPIANS 1:3–11 | I thank my God every time I remember you, constantly praying with joy in every one of my prayers for all of you, because of your sharing in the gospel from the first day until now. I am confident of this, that the one who began a good work among you will bring it to completion by the day of Jesus Christ. It is right for me to think this way about all of you, because you hold me in your heart, for all of you share in God's grace with me, both in my imprisonment and in the defense and confirmation of the gospel. For God is my witness, how I long for all of you with the compassion of Christ Jesus. And this is my prayer, that your love may overflow more and more with knowledge and full insight to help you to determine what is best, so that in the day of Christ you may be pure and blameless, having produced the harvest of righteousness that comes through Jesus Christ for the glory and praise of God.

Consider This

Repentance. How did such a good word get such a bad rap? The word *repent* conjures up decisively negative images of doomsday preachers shouting on street corners. It is largely associated with words like *stop, don't,* and *quit.* But what if the word is positive? What if repentance is more about turning toward something really good? What if it also means *go, do,* and *start*? It is one thing to turn away from something undesirable; it is quite another to turn to something beautiful. *Repent* means reorienting our highest aspirations toward the best thing imaginable. We were created for lives of inestimable goodness. Notice Paul's bold prayer from today's text:

And this is my prayer, that your love may overflow more and more with knowledge and full insight to help you to determine what is best.

That's what I want—my love overflowing more and more with knowledge and full insight to help me determine what is best. Said another way: I want to think like God thinks. Said another way: I want the same mind in me that was in Christ Jesus. Time for one more? How about, "Do not conform to the pattern of this world, but be transformed by the renewing of your mind. Then you will be able to test and approve what God's will is—his good, pleasing and perfect will" (Rom. 12:2 NIV).

Let's get fiercely practical. Your soul or inner life is like a garden. It responds to the law of reaping and sowing just like everything else in the universe—we reap what we sow. Here's the tricky part. Sow roses—reap roses. Sow tomatoes—reap tomatoes. Sow nothing—reap nothing. Right? Wrong! Sow nothing—reap weeds! We didn't even have to plant them. This is what Scripture means when it says we are sinful by nature. To be sure, repentance means weeding our souls, but even more so, it means sowing the seeds of incredible things. Remember yesterday's call about bearing fruits worthy of repentance? While weeding helps tons, fruit-bearing only comes from sowing new seeds.

Now watch how today's text wraps up with where this is all headed. It's all about *the harvest of righteousness that comes through Jesus Christ for the glory and praise of God.* Advent means repentance—pulling the weeds, but even more, sowing new seeds.

The Prayer

Our Father in heaven, nearer than my breath, thank you for these days of Advent and this new year in Christ. Thank you for this beautiful invitation to repent, to leave behind the futility of behavior management and to set my heart on the vision of a flourishing garden. Thank you that my life is not my project but yours. Come, Holy Spirit, and teach me how being transformed works differently than endlessly striving to transform myself. Show me the seeds to sow. In the name of Jesus Messiah—the one who came, is here, and is coming again—for his glory and our good, amen.

The Questions

- How is this Advent unfolding differently for you than in years past? Can you identify a seed you sense the Spirit wants to sow in your life today? Generosity, maybe? Patience?

The Train Wreck of Our Assumptions | 13

MATTHEW 11:2–11 | When John heard in prison what the Messiah was doing, he sent word by his disciples and said to him, "Are you the one who is to come, or are we to wait for another?" Jesus answered them, "Go and tell John what you hear and see: the blind receive their sight, the lame walk, the lepers are cleansed, the deaf hear, the dead are raised, and the poor have good news brought to them. And blessed is anyone who takes no offense at me."

As they went away, Jesus began to speak to the crowds about John: "What did you go out into the wilderness to look at? A reed shaken by the wind? What then did you go out to see?

Someone dressed in soft robes? Look, those who wear soft robes are in royal palaces. What then did you go out to see? A prophet? Yes, I tell you, and more than a prophet. This is the one about whom it is written,

'See, I am sending my messenger ahead of you,
who will prepare your way before you.'

Truly I tell you, among those born of women no one has arisen greater than John the Baptist; yet the least in the kingdom of heaven is greater than he."

Consider This

Questioning assumptions. That's what John was doing in that dank prison cell.

"Are you the one who is to come, or are we to wait for another?"

Our assumptions about how things should turn out can be blinding. Assumptions easily solidify into expectations. And expectations are the seeds of future bitterness. Divorce, cancer, bankruptcy, death, etc., weren't supposed to happen. We did everything right, followed Jesus, obeyed God's will. How can this be happening?

Isn't this John's quandary? The child of great promise, fore-runner of the Messiah, and prophet of greatest renown sits in a prison cell wondering if he wasted his life. Surely there has to be someone else coming. It looks to us like Jesus was hitting home runs, right? Look how he responded to John's question:

"Go and tell John what you hear and see: the blind receive their sight, the lame walk, the lepers are cleansed, the deaf hear,

the dead are raised, and the poor have good news brought to them. And blessed is anyone who takes no offense at me."

What more could a prophet want? I think John expected a lot more tables overturned, pink slips for high priests, revolting from Rome; more fireworks—less fluff; a little less conversation and a little more action. He expected something or someone else.

We are the same. We want God on our terms, or we don't want him at all. That's why so often it takes one of life's unforeseen train wrecks to open our eyes to the perspective of divine grace. We tend to meet up with God when we find ourselves backed into a corner with nowhere else to turn. These unwanted moments when we cannot change the reality we face offer the most profound possibilities of true life change. It may be precisely because the situation cannot change that everything else can change. Have you ever heard someone say cancer was the best thing that ever happened to them? They don't mean cancer was in any way good, just that awakening was better.

We find ourselves at about the halfway point in this Advent journey of awakening. We are equidistant from the starting gate and the finish line. We are, as noted earlier, somewhere in the middle of the beginning of the end. Might we question our assumptions about the second Advent of Jesus Christ? How might we examine our assumptions about Christmas and his first coming? Would we dare to ask ourselves an unthinkable question like: What if we are all asleep?

The Prayer

Our Father in heaven, nearer than my breath, thank you for these days of Advent and this new year in Christ. I hardly know where to start with this. My assumptions are like water to a fish. I don't even know how to get at them. I see what I see, which I fear blinds me to what you would like to show me. Maybe that is the place to start—with what I see and hear. Come, Holy Spirit, and give me eyes to see and ears to hear. Break in and break through. In the name of Jesus Messiah—the one who came, is here, and is coming again—for his glory and our good, amen.

The Question

- Would you be willing to ask yourself this question: What if I'm asleep?

14 True Gift-Giving Versus Reciprocation

1 THESSALONIANS 3:9–13 | How can we thank God enough for you in return for all the joy that we feel before our God because of you? Night and day we pray most earnestly that we may see you face to face and restore whatever is lacking in your faith.

Now may our God and Father himself and our Lord Jesus direct our way to you. And may the Lord make you increase and

abound in love for one another and for all, just as we abound in love for you. And may he so strengthen your hearts in holiness that you may be blameless before our God and Father at the coming of our Lord Jesus with all his saints.

Consider This

It's time to make the turn toward Christmas. Today's text identifies for us the deepest impulse of Christmas. Did you catch it?

And may the Lord make you increase and abound in love for one another and for all, just as we abound in love for you.

We experience at the heart of Christmas this deep impulse to "increase and abound in love for one another." It's why we want to give each other gifts. Something about all the commercialized retail madness threatens to change this holy impulse of abounding in love for one another into something altogether different. The word is *reciprocation*. Reciprocation lives in the world of social debt. Someone gives you a gift and you feel an obligation to reciprocate. It runs deep in the human race. It's not a bad thing; it's just not what Christmas is about. Underneath reciprocation lives expectation, which takes us away from the realm of love altogether and into the burden of meeting expectations. Reciprocation counterfeits love. Again, not a bad thing, but it is not "abounding love."

Christmas is all about the unutterably extravagant abounding love of God. The fullness of God comes to us in the frailty of an infant.

> For to us a child is born,
>> to us a son is given,
>> and the government will be on his shoulders.
> And he will be called
>> Wonderful Counselor, Mighty God,
>> Everlasting Father, Prince of Peace. (Isa. 9:6 NIV)

This is pure gift: abounding love. In the realm of abounding love, there is no reciprocation—only more love. The response to abounding love is not reciprocation but deep receiving leading to deepening relationship. Reciprocation is mostly about the giver meeting a requirement. Abounding love is always about the receiver. The difference is palpable.

I will forever remember a particular Christmas from my youth. My mother knew how to make Christmas an experience of abounding love. Her impulse was to give my two sisters and me something as over-the-top as the gift of Jesus on that first Christmas. On this particular Christmas Eve, which was always the timing of the gift, she passed out envelopes. Inside each envelope was a card on which was written a short rhyming poem. I will forever remember my card. It read, "You may want to keep it under keys and locks, but it's already in a pretty nice box. You know our love for you is great, the secret code is 2-8-4-8." My two sisters received similar rhymes also with numbers. We ran to our rooms to discover they had given each of us our own telephone and dedicated line. Mine was one of those phones in a wood-grained box that hinged open to reveal the dial pad and hand receiver. As a young teenager who lived for friends, this gift absolutely blew me away. I remember running back through the length of the house at top speed to embrace my mother with the most massive hug I had ever given her, probably before or since. In a spirit of abounding love, I said to her, "Thank you so much, Mom. I love you so much." Later that night, my dad pulled me aside and told me, "John David, you will never know how much your response to your mother's gift meant to her."

And may the Lord make you increase and abound in love for one another and for all, just as we abound in love for you.

The Prayer

Our Father in heaven, nearer than my breath, thank you for these days of Advent and this new year in Christ. I want to abound in love for others, yet I know my love for others will never compare to your abounding love for me. Wake me up to the extravagant and extraordinary love you have for me, not us, but *me*. I struggle to receive something I can't pay back. Come, Holy Spirit, and break through my brokenness into the childlike place in my heart. Break in and break through. In the name of Jesus Messiah—the one who came, is here, and is coming again—for his glory and our good, amen.

The Questions

- Why is it hard for you to freely receive a gift and not feel an impulse to reciprocate or pay back? What is that in us? Where does it come from?

15 Breaking Broken Attachments

LUKE 1:46–55 | And Mary said,
"My soul magnifies the Lord,
　and my spirit rejoices in God my Savior,
for he has looked with favor on the lowliness of his servant.
　Surely, from now on all generations will call me blessed;
for the Mighty One has done great things for me,
　and holy is his name.
His mercy is for those who fear him
　from generation to generation.
He has shown strength with his arm;
　he has scattered the proud in the thoughts of their hearts.
He has brought down the powerful from their thrones,
　and lifted up the lowly;
he has filled the hungry with good things,
　and sent the rich away empty.
He has helped his servant Israel,
　in remembrance of his mercy,
according to the promise he made to our ancestors,
　to Abraham and to his descendants forever."

Consider This

The miracle happened in Mary's body. The ancient Creed of the Apostles rings out, "I believe in Jesus Christ, his only Son, our Lord; conceived by the Holy Spirit, born of the Virgin

Mary." The Holy Spirit conceived Jesus, the Son of God, in Mary's womb. The miracle also happened in Mary's soul. We see it in today's text:

"My soul magnifies the Lord, and my spirit rejoices in God my Savior, for he has looked with favor on the lowliness of his servant."

Whatever our soul magnifies, our spirit reacts and responds to. God crafted the human soul for the purpose of magnifying himself alone. Only as my soul magnifies the Lord does my spirit truly rejoice. Everything else we might call "rejoicing" is ephemeral happiness riding on the rising tide of favorable circumstances. This is perhaps the hardest lesson in life. It's what leads us to chase whatever we think will make us happy. Our spirit is ever in search of something to quench its thirst, to make it soar, to find its song, restless until we learn to rejoice in God our Savior. This only happens as our soul learns to magnify the Lord. It requires an awakening. Our spirit is in search of the deepest, most holy, most beautiful attachment imaginable; the relationship for which we were made and through which all other relationships can flourish.

It's why during the holidays more people drink more alcohol than ever. Awakening feels too threatening. It means facing the brokenness in our present, which stems from the brokenness in our past. It is easier to numb our spirit with some other spirit (i.e., alcohol) in an effort to cover over whatever it is the broken glass of our soul has chosen to magnify. It's why people have more extramarital affairs during the holidays. In our quiet desperation we will settle for a thousand unholy attachments, all of them promising a life none of them can deliver.

When my soul magnifies the Lord, it reveals the holiest of all attachments, and it opens the way for holiness (which is true happiness) in all of our attachments—to our own selves, our families, our friends, even our enemies. It's why at the core of our faith stands a singular command: "Love the Lord your God with all your heart, and with all your soul, and with all your mind" and "love your neighbor as yourself" (Matt. 22:37, 39). These are the movements of a soul who is learning to magnify the Lord. Broken attachments are mended. Unholy attachments are cast off. As my soul magnifies the Lord, my wounded spirit is delivered from every bondage, healed, and set free to rejoice.

The Prayer

Our Father in heaven, nearer than my breath, thank you for these days of Advent and this new year in Christ. Thank you for this hard but beautiful teaching. Show me what my soul is magnifying. Gently awaken me to the broken places in the magnifying glass of my soul. Something about these holidays has a way of bringing the pain to the surface. Transform them into holy days where I resist my impulse to cover it over and instead become vulnerable before you, the lover of my soul. Come, Holy Spirit, and train my soul to magnify the Lord, and teach my spirit to rejoice in God my Savior. In the name of Jesus Messiah—the one who came, is here, and is coming again—for his glory and our good, amen.

The Questions
- How is today's text and reflection speaking to you? Do you sense awakening near? Don't be afraid. Lean in.

The Refreshing Relief of Holiness

16

ISAIAH 35:1–10 NIV | The desert and the parched land will be glad; the wilderness will rejoice and blossom.
Like the crocus, it will burst into bloom;
    it will rejoice greatly and shout for joy.
The glory of Lebanon will be given to it,
    the splendor of Carmel and Sharon;
they will see the glory of the LORD,
    the splendor of our God.

Strengthen the feeble hands,
    steady the knees that give way;
say to those with fearful hearts,
    "Be strong, do not fear;
your God will come,
    he will come with vengeance;
with divine retribution
    he will come to save you."

Then will the eyes of the blind be opened
    and the ears of the deaf unstopped.

Then will the lame leap like a deer,
and the mute tongue shout for joy.
Water will gush forth in the wilderness
and streams in the desert.
The burning sand will become a pool,
the thirsty ground bubbling springs.
In the haunts where jackals once lay,
grass and reeds and papyrus will grow.

And a highway will be there;
it will be called the Way of Holiness;
it will be for those who walk on that Way.
The unclean will not journey on it;
wicked fools will not go about on it.
No lion will be there,
nor any ravenous beast;
they will not be found there.
But only the redeemed will walk there,
and those the Lord has rescued will return.
They will enter Zion with singing;
everlasting joy will crown their heads.
Gladness and joy will overtake them,
and sorrow and sighing will flee away.

Consider This

There are two gigantic words in Scripture that most aptly describe God. These two words are larger than all of the cathedrals on earth combined can hold or even fathom. The words: *holy* and *love*.

Let's begin with *holy*. Holiness. You may not have noticed, but some form of the word appears seventy times through these Advent pages. For many of us, the word smacks of a religious program we are wholly uninterested in. It feels like an old nun at Catholic school with a ruler in her hands poised to crack someone's knuckles if they so much as look like they are having fun. We think it means something like good behavior on steroids. Even the way Bible teachers describe holiness as "being set apart" misses the point. It's not wrong, but it's not quite right either. It just feels too much like a group of people who are off to themselves in some kind of quarantine because they don't want to catch the sin virus everyone else has but them. The great irony of this brand of so-called holiness is that no one wants to go near it.

What if holiness is not immunity from the world, but the contagion in the world we want everyone to catch? What if holiness means to be set apart like the late Kobe Bryant was set apart when he had a basketball in his hands, inspiring awe and amazement? Or like Mozart arranging notes on a page? What if holiness means being set apart like Jesus doing all the things he did and still does, like rubbing shoulders with lepers and pardoning prostitutes? What if holiness is a kind of greatness that inspires greatness, and not only inspires it but empowers it?

What if holiness is not what we thought? What if holiness means blind eyes open, deaf ears hearing, lame people leaping, and mute tongues singing? What if holiness means water springing up in the desert, pools of refreshment in the place of arid sand? If so, this means holiness is actually relief; a reversal of broken conditions and situations. This means holiness is love.

It brings us to that second gigantic word to describe God: *love*. The way of holiness looks like a viral movement of concentrated love.

The Prayer

Our Father in heaven, nearer than my breath, thank you for these days of Advent and this new year in Christ. Thank you, for your holiness is filled with love and your love is filled with holiness. Thank you for the way your Spirit brings these two divine realities into a single union. Come, Holy Spirit, and make the holy love of God the very substance of my life and character, so much so that my presence exudes your presence and becomes your power through my very being. I abandon myself to you. In the name of Jesus Messiah—the one who came, is here, and is coming again—for his glory and our good, amen.

The Questions

- Have you ever connected the words *holy* and *love* and thought of them as a singular reality? If not, why not? What impact do they have on each other for you? How does it change your notion of the word *holiness*? Of *love*?

Hurry Up and Wait

17

PSALM 25:1–10 | To you, O LORD, I lift up my soul.
O my God, in you I trust;
   do not let me be put to shame;
   do not let my enemies exult over me.
Do not let those who wait for you be put to shame;
   let them be ashamed who are wantonly treacherous.

Make me to know your ways, O LORD;
   teach me your paths.
Lead me in your truth, and teach me,
   for you are the God of my salvation;
   for you I wait all day long.

Be mindful of your mercy, O LORD, and of your steadfast love,
   for they have been from of old.
Do not remember the sins of my youth or my transgressions;
   according to your steadfast love remember me,
   for your goodness' sake, O LORD!

Good and upright is the LORD;
   therefore he instructs sinners in the way.
He leads the humble in what is right,
   and teaches the humble his way.
All the paths of the LORD are steadfast love and faithfulness,
   for those who keep his covenant and his decrees.

Consider This

Have you ever waited for that call from the doctor's office with the results of a test? Have you ever waited for hours in miles of stalled traffic on the interstate? What about waiting in the checkout lines at the retail outlets within a week of Christmas? How about waiting for three entire minutes for a traffic light to turn? Have you ever waited for more than thirty seconds for a website to load on the Internet?

Why do we hate to wait? Is it that we are too busy or too important? Waiting takes us out of control of the situation. Waiting reminds us that someone else is in control. Waiting humbles us. What if the "paths of the Lord" are more about pace than destination? What if our days became exercises in waiting on the Lord, as in, "for you I wait all day long"? How about we take all those occasions in the coming days where we find ourselves waiting and we consider in the midst of it all that we are waiting on the Lord.

Think about it. The people of God waited for four hundred years to hear from God. That's almost two times the age of the United States. It means multiple generations of people lived and died without any word from God beyond the prophet Malachi. They waited. They held on to the prophecies and passed the torch of the promises to their children's children. Before that, the Israelites waited hundreds of years in Egypt for the deliverance of God.

We live in the age of the Holy Spirit, the span of history between the two Advents of Jesus. It has been more than two thousand years on our clocks; only a few days in the Lord's time as noted earlier. We are waiting. In the age of the Spirit, he is actively speaking and moving and bringing the firstfruits of the kingdom of heaven among us. We don't wait passively but actively. This season of Advent offers the wake-up call to reactivate our waiting muscles, to lift our eyes to the horizon and put our hands to the plow. Don't worry if you have drifted off a bit or lost your footing and traction. The time has come to get back up, dust off, and get back in the game. It sounds wrong, but the old adage "hurry up and wait" is exactly right. There is perhaps no more biblical call to the people of God than to wait for the Lord. "Wait for the LORD; be strong and take heart and wait for the LORD" (Ps. 27:14 NIV).

The Prayer

Our Father in heaven, nearer than my breath, thank you for these days of Advent and this new year in Christ. I confess I do not like to wait. Turn the everyday occurrences of waiting on this or that into holy reminders to work out the spiritual muscles of my soul. I need heart-level transformation. Train my spirit to shift from anxiety to anticipation. Come, Holy Spirit, infuse me with the patience of God Almighty, whose timing is always perfect. In the name of Jesus Messiah—the one who came, is here, and is coming again—for his glory and our good, amen.

The Questions

- What is it about you that is put off by having to wait for someone? Do you get angry when someone is late? What is going on underneath these feelings?

18 Dealing with Our Anxiety

PHILIPPIANS 4:4–7 NIV | Rejoice in the Lord always. I will say it again: Rejoice! Let your gentleness be evident to all. The Lord is near. Do not be anxious about anything, but in every situation, by prayer and petition, with thanksgiving, present your requests to God. And the peace of God, which transcends all understanding, will guard your hearts and your minds in Christ Jesus.

Consider This

Anxiety may be one of the biggest issues of our time. It robs us of so many things. What is anxiety? The *Oxford Dictionary* defines anxiety as "a feeling of worry, nervousness, or unease, typically about an imminent event or something with an uncertain outcome." Psychiatry defines anxiety as "a nervous disorder characterized by a state of excessive uneasiness and apprehension, typically with compulsive behavior or panic attacks." Anxiety is common to humanity; it lives on a spectrum and we know it when we feel it. But what is it, really? Here's my take: anxiety is the felt experience of being unaware of the presence of God.

Today's text tells us, "Do not be anxious about anything." Translation: be aware of the presence of God in all things all the time.

On a sheet of paper, make two columns. Label the left column: "Things That Are Bringing Me Joy." Label the right column: "Things That Are Causing Me Anxiety." Take a few minutes to reflect and list out everything you can think of in those two columns. You have likely not done this in a while. You may have never done it at all. It is so important to get these things out of the shadows of our lives and into the light. Start with the left column and read them aloud.

Now one at a time, say, "Father, I thank you for _____, and I rejoice in you. Again, I take joy in you." Rejoicing in the Lord has a way of magnifying our blessings and joy. Now read the list on the right column aloud one at a time as a prayer to God. "Father, I give you _____, and I ask you to _____."

Now come back to the second verse of today's Advent text, hidden in plain sight between verses 4 and 6: "Let your gentleness be evident to all. The Lord is near." It's right there between rejoicing always and not being anxious. In the wake of this work, note the gentleness with which the Spirit is calming your being. We are empty of anxiety and full of joy. This is the life God intends for us to live all the time.

The Prayer

Our Father in heaven, nearer than my breath, thank you for these days of Advent and this new year in Christ. This all seems so clear and yet so far from me a lot of the time. Train my spirit to rejoice in the Lord, no matter what. I confess my training is to rejoice in good circumstances and happy times more than I have learned to rejoice in the Lord. It means I get depressed in the face of difficult circumstances. Teach me this way of rejoicing that burns off anxiety like a morning fog. Come, Holy Spirit, infuse me with the gentleness that comes from your nearness. In the name of Jesus Messiah—the one who came, is here, and is coming again—for his glory and our good, amen.

The Question

- Anxiety is the felt experience of being unaware of the presence of God. How do you relate to this statement from today's reflection?

19 Naming Our Holy Discontent

JEREMIAH 33:14–16 | The days are surely coming, says the LORD, when I will fulfill the promise I made to the house of Israel and the house of Judah. In those days and at that time I will cause a righteous Branch to spring up for David; and he shall execute justice and righteousness in the land. In those days Judah will be saved and Jerusalem will live in safety. And this is the name by which it will be called: "The LORD is our righteousness."

Consider This

Holy discontent. That's when it begins. When we can finally be honest enough with ourselves to say something like, "There must be more to life than this," or, "I'm sick and tired of being sick and tired," or, "I have everything I ever wanted, but I still haven't found what I'm looking for." Our contentment with that which does not satisfy slowly lulls us into a slumber many never awaken from. Holy discontent may be the best gift prosperity can give us, for it cracks the door to the kind of room we thought was too good to be true.

It's time to name it. Stop denying that gnawing sense of need just beneath the surface. Stop feeding it with more food or drink or entertainment or toys or trips or new companions. This only increases our appetite for the things that can never satisfy. The difference between a crisis and an awakening is the way we deal with our discontent. It can lead us to holy ground or drive us into the pit of hell.

This is why the holidays can be so difficult for so many. There comes a point in life when sentimental songs can no longer cover over the unintended consequences of the unattended pain of the past. Something about the holidays wakes people up in a way that induces even deeper slumber. It becomes a season of unbridled consumption as though the emptiness could be filled with food and drink and things all covered with wrapping paper and twinkling lights. What if this is merely the mask of Christmas, and what if Advent is the opportunity to gently take it off? We fear the feeling of emptiness just below the surface so we keep ourselves full with the things that cannot fulfill. Just under that unperceived yet feared emptiness dwells the gift of holy discontent. Might we let it shift from a dull gnawing into a crystallized reality? It opens the door to Advent's awakening.

We are more than the sum of our unfulfilled longings. In fact, our deepest longing of all is for someone to make it all okay—no, not just okay, but deeply right. We long for transcendence, for someone beyond us to come in and make life right again.

And this is the name by which it will be called: "The Lord *is our righteousness."*

Righteousness may not be the opposite of bad behavior after all. It is the deepest remedy for what is wrong. Righteousness means life made right again—not by our efforts but from beyond us.

Take a minute today and complete this sentence in writing: "The thing I am truly longing for in my life is . . ."

The Prayer

Our Father in heaven, nearer than my breath, thank you for these days of Advent and this new year in Christ. Something about this bothers me, yet I know it is right. I confess I push out and press down this gnawing sense of things not being right deep down. I feel burdened to fix things and I know I can't, so I do my best to cover it over and press on. I am ready to name it, Lord. This is the gift of holy discontent. I will name it. Come, Holy Spirit, let this discontent be crystallized in such a way leading to a transcendent breakthrough of your life in mine. In the name of Jesus Messiah—the one who came, is here, and is coming again—for his glory and our good, amen.

The Question

- Stay with the inquiry: "The thing I am truly longing for in my life is . . ."

The Watchword of All Watchwords

20

ISAIAH 7:10–16 NIV | Again the LORD spoke to Ahaz, "Ask the LORD your God for a sign, whether in the deepest depths or in the highest heights."

But Ahaz said, "I will not ask; I will not put the LORD to the test."

Then Isaiah said, "Hear now, you house of David! Is it not enough to try the patience of humans? Will you try the patience of my God also?

Therefore the Lord himself will give you a sign: [BEHOLD!] The virgin will conceive and give birth to a son, and will call him Immanuel. He will be eating curds and honey when he knows enough to reject the wrong and choose the right, for before the boy knows enough to reject the wrong and choose the right, the land of the two kings you dread will be laid waste.

Consider This

Over the days leading up to Christmas, a watchword will present itself in clear fashion. The word? *Behold*. The Greek word we translate as "behold" is *idou*. In most instances, the short Greek word *idou* is simply not translated. For some reason, many modern translators of the most popular versions of the Bible have chosen to leave this word out of our English versions. Can you see the irony? The word meant to alert us to pay special attention to what follows is omitted. Might this, in part, explain some of our failure to acknowledge the vast depth of certain occasions? We no longer look when we think we have seen; hence our need to be reminded over and again to "behold!" In order for you, the reader, to feel the effect of this curious and critical omission, I have elected to insert the omitted word as "Behold!" It is intended to have a jarring effect.

Behold is a very important word. It has the effect of a group of children standing in the middle of a busy intersection wildly waving their arms in order to stop traffic and get passersby to pay attention to what is unfolding just off the well-worn path.

This tiny, overlooked Bible word means "to pay attention," bringing every faculty of our perception into submission to the events unfolding in the world-making wonder of the Word of God. It is the watchword of all watchwords.

Christmas is all at once a sign both in the deepest depths and the highest heights. Advent prepares us for the apparent contradiction.

A virgin with child? For her, that would be the deepest depths. Pregnant with the Son of God by the power of the Holy Spirit? For us, that would be the highest heights.

"Glory to God in the highest" (Luke 2:14), the angels will soon sing, because glory came down to the lowest—as they invited lowly shepherds to be the first visitors. Christmas will show us in sketch what the cross will reveal in full technicolor: a sign both in the deepest depths and the highest heights.

This word from the prophet Isaiah comes to mind: "Behold, I am doing a new thing; now it springs forth, do you not perceive it? I will make a way in the wilderness and rivers in the desert" (Isa. 43:19 ESV). Jesus is the new thing. It's why Scripture says, "Therefore, if anyone is in Christ, he is a new creation. The old has passed away; behold, the new has come" (2 Cor. 5:17 ESV). Did you catch it there? "Behold, the new has come." All the way to the end and beyond, Jesus is the new thing. "And he who was seated on the throne said, 'Behold, I am making all things new.' Also he said, 'Write this down, for these words are trustworthy and true'" (Rev. 21:5 ESV). Did you catch it again? "Behold, I am making all things new."

The invitation is to behold. It is Advent's way of saying, "Wake up!"

The Prayer

Our Father in heaven, nearer than my breath, thank you for these days of Advent and this new year in Christ. Thank you for this watchword: *behold*. I want to learn to behold, to see beyond the surface of what I think I've seen before. Teach me not to simply look at things but to see into them. Shake me awake in these days leading up to Christmas. Awaken me to the new creation work Jesus is doing and wants to do in me, in my family, and in the world. Come, Holy Spirit, illuminate my heart and mind. Give me eyes to see and ears to hear. In the name of Jesus Messiah—the one who came, is here, and is coming again—for his glory and our good, amen.

The Questions

- What will it take in this last week leading up to Christmas to shift your faculties of perception from distraction to attention? How might you begin beholding in a new way?

21 Revisit First Things: Faith and Prayer

LUKE 1:26–38 | In the sixth month the angel Gabriel was sent by God to a town in Galilee called Nazareth, to a virgin engaged to a man whose name was Joseph, of the house of David. The virgin's name was Mary. And he came to her and said, "Greetings, favored one! The Lord is with you." But she was much perplexed by his words and pondered what sort of greeting this might be. The angel said to her, "Do not be afraid, Mary, for you have found favor with God. [Behold!], you will conceive in your womb and bear a son, and you will name him Jesus. He will be great, and will be called the Son of the Most High, and the Lord God will give to him the throne of his ancestor David. He will reign over the house of Jacob forever, and of his kingdom there will be no end." Mary said to the angel, "How can this be, since I am a virgin?" The angel said to her, "The Holy Spirit will come upon you, and the power of the Most High will overshadow you; therefore the child to be born will be holy; he will be called Son of God. [Behold!,] your relative Elizabeth in her old age has also conceived a son; and this is the sixth month for her who was said to be barren. For nothing will be impossible with God." Then Mary said, "[Behold!] Here am I, the servant of the Lord; let it be with me according to your word." Then the angel departed from her.

Consider This

I wonder if he thought he had the address wrong. Gabriel must have looked sideways at the directions. Nazareth? He was looking for a teenaged girl, Mary, to whom he would announce the coming of the Messiah—to be conceived by the Holy Spirit in her womb and born through her virgin body.

History calls it the annunciation. I never understood that word. It always felt like the inaccessible terminology of some distant theological doctrine. Why didn't they just call it "The Announcement?" That's what it means. Why do we need a big-city word for a small-town story? Gabriel didn't go to Jerusalem or Athens or Rome. He went to Nazareth, a place of apparent insignificance. Later, upon hearing Jesus is from Nazareth, Nathanael will remark, "Can anything good come out of Nazareth?" (John 1:46).

God chooses the apparently insignificant to accomplish the impossible. Cities matter to God, but he seems to reserve something special for small towns. More people live in cities, but there are a whole lot more small towns. There's something about small-town life that fosters big-time faith. Behold the announcement:

"Do not be afraid, Mary, for you have found favor with God. [Behold!], you will conceive in your womb and bear a son, and you will name him Jesus. He will be great, and will be called the Son of the Most High, and the Lord God will give to him the throne of his ancestor David."

Behold the faith of the handmaiden of the Lord, Mary. She dares to question the angel:

"How can this be, since I am a virgin?"

Behold the unprecedented nature of the angel's impossible answer:

"The Holy Spirit will come upon you, and the power of the Most High will overshadow you; therefore the child to be born will be holy; he will be called Son of God."

Behold the angel's bold declaration:

"For nothing will be impossible with God."

Behold Mary's bold and unflinching prayerful declaration of faith:

"[Behold!] Here am I, the servant of the Lord; let it be with me according to your word."

This is small-town faith in a big-time God. In fact, if we had to boil this whole thing down to two essentials, I think these would be the two:

1. Faith: "Nothing will be impossible with God."
2. Prayer: "Let it be with me according to your word."

Bottom line today: he has your zip code too. Small town or big city, he has your zip code. Just remember, faith says yes before the assignment comes. It comes down to faith and prayer. Start practicing now. Faith: nothing will be impossible with God. Prayer: let it be with me according to your word.

The Prayer

Our Father in heaven, nearer than my breath, thank you for these days of Advent and this new year in Christ. Faith and prayer, that's all I need. Here is my faith, Lord Jesus: nothing will be impossible with you. And here is my prayer: may it be with me according to your word. Come, Holy Spirit, and train me in these stunningly simple and ever-deepening essentials of faith and prayer. In the name of Jesus Messiah—the one who came, is here, and is coming again—for his glory and our good, amen.

The Questions

• Will you write these two essentials down today: faith and prayer? Nothing will be impossible with God. Let it be with me according to your word. How can these go forward with you?

22 Do Hard Things

MATTHEW 1:18–25 | Now the birth of Jesus the Messiah took place in this way. When his mother Mary had been engaged to Joseph, but before they lived together, she was found to be with child from the Holy Spirit. Her husband Joseph, being a righteous man and unwilling to expose her to public disgrace, planned to dismiss her quietly. But just when he had resolved to do this, [behold!,] an angel of the Lord appeared to him in a dream and said, "Joseph, son of David, do not be afraid to take Mary as your wife, for the child conceived in her is from the Holy Spirit. She will bear a son, and you are to name him Jesus, for he will save his people from their sins." All this took place to fulfill what had been spoken by the Lord through the prophet:

"[Behold!,] the virgin shall conceive and bear a son,
    and they shall name him Emmanuel,"

which means, "God is with us." When Joseph awoke from sleep, he did as the angel of the Lord commanded him; he took her as his wife, but had no marital relations with her until she had borne a son; and he named him Jesus.

Consider This

The story of Christmas has absolutely zero in common with our snow globe nativity set. Consider Joseph. Here was an ordinary guy, excited about marrying the girl of his dreams. And in an afternoon, everything imploded. In his mind, it was over. The dignified exit strategy was all but done. Then there was the dream.

"Joseph, son of David, do not be afraid to take Mary as your wife, for the child conceived in her is from the Holy Spirit. She will bear a son, and you are to name him Jesus, for he will save his people from their sins."

Joseph did the hard thing. Life would not get easier. His hope for a normal life was over. Later would come yet another dream warning him to take his family and leave the country to avoid genocide. This son who was not his son would cost him everything. Joseph died to his dreams for the sake of the greater dream. Joseph, without doubt, is the most under-rated and under-celebrated member of the cast of the story of Jesus. He did the hard thing.

We live in an age where even premarital purity seems too hard for many. In light of this, notice Joseph's purity after their marriage ceremony:

When Joseph awoke from sleep, he did as the angel of the Lord commanded him; he took her as his wife, but had no marital relations with her until she had borne a son; and he named him Jesus.

Were he among us, he would likely offer us this advice: "Do hard things. It's worth it. And remember, sometimes what seems to be righteous may not always be right."

The Prayer

Our Father in heaven, nearer than my breath, thank you for these days of Advent and this new year in Christ. In an age where I am pulled down by the gravity of such low standards and lowest-common-denominator faith, let me remember Joseph. Prepare my faith to do hard things, to make courageous decisions, and to let the outcome of good faith and hard things be its own reward. Come, Holy Spirit, and build this character in me that my legacy might point others to Jesus. In the name of Jesus Messiah—the one who came, is here, and is coming again—for his glory and our good, amen.

The Questions

- When is the last time you had to exercise good faith to do a hard thing? How did that go? What do you notice and appreciate about Joseph in this Advent season?

23 Getting into the Christmas Spirit

LUKE 1:39–45 | In those days Mary set out and went with haste to a Judean town in the hill country, where she entered the house of Zechariah and greeted Elizabeth. When Elizabeth heard Mary's greeting, the child leaped in her womb. And Elizabeth was filled with the Holy Spirit and exclaimed with a loud cry, "Blessed are you among women, and blessed is the fruit of your womb. And why has this happened to me, that the mother of my Lord comes to me? For [behold!] as soon as I heard the sound of your greeting, the child in my womb leaped for joy. And blessed is she who believed that there would be a fulfillment of what was spoken to her by the Lord."

Consider This

The closer we get to Christmas, the more prose must give way to poems. It's why singing figures so prominently at this time of year. Think about it. When in life are more people singing more of the very same songs more of the time than ever in the entire year? Christian or not, just about everybody loves Christmas music. Why? It's because like no other time, the music of Christmas unites us. During Advent, the season preceding Christmas, we all listen to the very same songs—every single year, without fail—together. In fact, radio stations start playing Christmas music before Thanksgiving, and for some of them, it's all they play around the clock. Shopping malls are like a symphony from the common songs in the concourses to the cacophony of medleys coming from the individual stores. From "O Little Town of Bethlehem" and "Away in a Manger" to "White Christmas," there really is no sacred/secular divide at Christmas. No matter how commercialized and materialistic the season becomes, Christmas still belongs to Jesus.

Everyone loves to get into the Christmas spirit. And what exactly is "the Christmas spirit"? Can we be honest? The Christmas spirit is the Holy Spirit. From the day of Pentecost forward, the Holy Spirit courses across the face of the earth, moving with the awakening energy of heaven on earth, ever ready to invade and embrace anyone and everyone with the miracle of Jesus Messiah. In this one-of-its-kind season, the Spirit's prevenient, preparatory work is remarkably present and public. At Christmas, the whole world is showing up at our party, singing our songs, and more open-hearted to the possibilities of God breaking in on their brokenness than in the rest of the calendar year combined. For Christians, the Christmas spirit must increasingly mean being filled with the Holy Spirit in ways making us radically hospitable, boldly open, extraordinarily generous, and deeply attuned to the ways Jesus wants to work within, among, and through us. No matter how crazy the holiday party gets, Jesus owns Christmas. In fact, Jesus is Christmas.

When Elizabeth heard Mary's greeting, the child leaped in her womb. And Elizabeth was filled with the Holy Spirit and exclaimed with a loud cry, "Blessed are you among women, and blessed is the fruit of your womb."

Look what happened in this story. Mary shows up carrying Jesus in her womb. The child in Elizabeth's womb leaps for joy at the awareness of the prenatal presence of Jesus, and Elizabeth is filled with the Holy Spirit! This is a profound awakening story.

What if it could be like that for us? We, like pregnant Mary, carry Jesus. (Really, it's more like Jesus carries us.) As we move about in the open and joyful air of the holiday season, instead of lamenting that Christmas is everywhere and Jesus is nowhere, what if we focused on the fact that we carry Jesus? And what if we carried the faith—that as we carry Jesus—something deep in others leaps for joy at the awareness of his presence? The Holy Spirit stands present and ever ready to kindle awareness of and attunement to Jesus in every person on earth. What if the Spirit is waiting on us to show up with Jesus—to our party—even at someone else's house? How's that for getting into the Christmas spirit?

The Prayer

Our Father in heaven, nearer than my breath, thank you for these days of Advent and this new year in Christ. Lord Jesus, Christmas belongs to you and yet you want it to belong to the whole world. Make me a true bearer of your presence, the real Christmas spirit, as I move about these festive days. Come, Holy Spirit, and attune me to the longings unaware that the people all around me are carrying within them. Be so alive in me that others leap for joy at your presence within me. In the name of Jesus Messiah—the one who came, is here, and is coming again—for his glory and our good, amen.

The Questions

- Are you ready to take Jesus with you into the Christmas celebration? How can it be different this time around? How will you be different? How will Jesus be different in and through you?

24 Letting Go of Our Security Blanket

LUKE 2:1–20 NIV | In those days Caesar Augustus issued a decree that a census should be taken of the entire Roman world. (This was the first census that took place while Quirinius was governor of Syria.) And everyone went to their own town to register.

So Joseph also went up from the town of Nazareth in Galilee to Judea, to Bethlehem the town of David, because he belonged to the house and line of David. He went there to register with Mary, who was pledged to be married to him and was expecting a child. While they were there, the time came for the baby to be born, and she gave birth to her firstborn, a son. She wrapped him in cloths and placed him in a manger, because there was no guest room available for them.

And there were shepherds living out in the fields nearby, keeping watch over their flocks at night. An angel of the Lord appeared to them, and the glory of the Lord shone around them, and they were terrified. But the angel said to them, "Do not be afraid. [Behold!] I bring you good news that will cause great joy for all the people. Today in the town of David a Savior has been born to you; he is the Messiah, the Lord. This will be a sign to you: You will find a baby wrapped in cloths and lying in a manger."

Suddenly a great company of the heavenly host appeared with the angel, praising God and saying,

"Glory to God in the highest heaven,
and on earth peace to those on whom his favor rests."

When the angels had left them and gone into heaven, the shepherds said to one another, "Let's go to Bethlehem and see this thing that has happened, which the Lord has told us about."

So they hurried off and found Mary and Joseph, and the baby, who was lying in the manger. When they had seen him, they spread the word concerning what had been told them about this child, and all who heard it were amazed at what the shepherds said to them. But Mary treasured up all these things and pondered them in her heart. The shepherds returned, glorifying and praising God for all the things they had heard and seen, which were just as they had been told.

Consider This

I can't help but hear this text in the voice of Linus, the brother of Lucy and friend of Charlie Brown, from the late Charles Schultz's celebrated cartoon strip *Peanuts*. Linus recites the text as his part in the annual Christmas play in the animated television classic, *A Charlie Brown Christmas*.

The big story in the Charlie Brown Christmas story is how nothing works out as planned and yet things still go according to plan. There are *our* plans and then there is always the bigger plan we can't fully see. Most of the time it takes the interruption of our best-laid plans for the bigger plan to happen.

Linus was known for his security blanket. Though he grew older, he would not let go of his baby blanket. He always carried the blanket and sucked his thumb. The blanket itself became a kind of character throughout all the years of the *Peanuts* comic strip with all of the other characters developing their own postures (from ambivalent to aggressive) toward it and Linus's dependency.

We all have security blankets. We are all attached to something or someone. No matter how difficult, delightful, prosperous, or poor our conditions become, we all crave the comfort of predictable lives. For some, the security blanket is a well-funded 401k; for others, it is a daily package of cigarettes or a nightly bottle of wine. For many, security comes in the form of a tangled web of codependent relationships, requiring us to constantly contort ourselves to please one and perform for another. In one way or another, visible or not, most of us carry a security blanket, something to cover ourselves when we feel vulnerable.

It's what's so amazing about Christmas Eve. These shepherds, Bedouin farmers, were at the low end of the societal spectrum. They wandered around the countryside scratching out a living for their families from the herd of sheep. They lived out their lives, like the vast majority of everyone else who has ever lived in this world, in the stable insecurity of a predictable poverty. It was to these God first declared the birth of his Son. He went to the ones with the smallest security blanket in order to lead them to a baby wrapped in swaddling clothes and lying in a feeding trough with no security blanket at all.

But the angel said to them, "Do not be afraid. [Behold!] I bring you good news that will cause great joy for all the people. Today in the town of David a Savior has been born to you; he is the Messiah, the Lord.

This is the security that ends all insecurity. This is the covering beyond which any blanket can provide. And this sign, "You will find a baby wrapped in cloths and lying in a manger," a demonstration of great vulnerability, turns out to be the greatest security. Jesus saves completely, totally, and comprehensively from this first Advent through the final Advent. Nothing is more secure and no one is more protected than when she is wrapped in the life-filled, love-soaked covering of the Lamb of God.

Schultz was a Christian and he wanted the Charlie Brown Christmas special to be about Jesus; after all, the story is about Charlie Brown's search for the real meaning of the holiday. The television producers balked at the idea. Schultz won in the end by writing into the script this "Christmas play" moment with Linus reciting verbatim the Christmas story from Luke's Gospel. And, what do you know, he even dropped in a little Easter egg for those with eyes to see. About midway through Linus's reading, he drops his well-worn security blanket on the floor. Enough said. Christmas belongs to Jesus, and all Jesus wants for Christmas is for us, you and me, to belong to him.

The Prayer

Our Father in heaven, nearer than my breath, thank you for these days of Advent and this new year in Christ. Thank you for the shepherds, likely wrapped in worn-out rags as clothing, and for telling them first. Thank you for showing them the sign of a baby wrapped in swaddling clothes and lying in a manger—the very Savior of the whole world. I confess, I am tired of my endless efforts to stabilize my security. It keeps me in a predictability that counterfeits real life. Come, Holy Spirit, and awaken me to the miracle. Give me the grace to drop the security I cling to, which is really only insecurity. I want to take hold of you this time around, because I know you will never let me go. In the name of Jesus Messiah—the one who came, is here, and is coming again—for his glory and our good, amen.

The Questions

- Where does your security come from? And how does this source reveal your insecurity? How might you let go of the security that is insecurity and take hold of the vulnerable security of Jesus Christ?

25 Born Again on Christmas Day

JOHN 1:1–14 NIV | In the beginning was the Word, and the Word was with God, and the Word was God. He was with God in the beginning. Through him all things were made; without him nothing was made that has been made. In him was life, and that life was the light of all mankind. The light shines in the darkness, and the darkness has not overcome it.

There was a man sent from God whose name was John. He came as a witness to testify concerning that light, so that through him all might believe. He himself was not the light; he came only as a witness to the light.

The true light that gives light to everyone was coming into the world. He was in the world, and though the world was made through him, the world did not recognize him. He came to that which was his own, but his own did not receive him. Yet to all who did receive him, to those who believed in his name, he gave the right to become children of God—children born not of natural descent, nor of human decision or a husband's will, but born of God.

The Word became flesh and made his dwelling among us. We have seen his glory, the glory of the one and only Son, who came from the Father, full of grace and truth.

Consider This

"Christmas is for children," or, "Christmas brings out the child in us all." Those are nice sentimental thoughts on one level, but might they hold a more serious truth? Could Christmas be for adults too?

On more than one occasion while teaching about his kingdom, Jesus lifted up a child and said things like, "Whoever wants to enter into the kingdom of heaven must become like a child" (e.g., Matt. 18:3; Mark 10:15; Luke 18:17). This has most often been interpreted in a sentimental fashion, lifting out the whimsical, wondrous, carefree nature of children as the prerequisite mentality for entering into God's kingdom. While these are commendable qualities, and perhaps have a modicum of relevance to what Jesus was saying, the biblical evidence points to a different meaning. In the first century, children held no status or value in the community. Children were more like slaves in the sense of being the property of another with no status or social value of their own.

While this is far from the case for most children in our North American context, it remains the situation for millions of children around the world. Many of them find themselves as both status-less children and slaves. Jesus' point was not to become carefree and whimsical, which would have been somewhat foreign concepts to a first-century child. He lifted up a child to reference his utter humility. In the eyes of the society, they brought nothing to the table of value; not even themselves. Here's a rough translation: "Unless you become humble, like this child, coming to grips with the fact that you bring nothing to the table, no claim of entitlement, no rights (birthrights or otherwise), privileges, status or anything else; unless you humble yourself in this fashion, just like this child I hold up before you, and enter in on the very same level as anyone else, you can't come in. It's not because I am barring the door to hold you out. It's because you are disqualifying yourselves from even the possibility of perceiving the reality of my kingdom to begin with."

With this backdrop, hear the Christmas text again:

Yet to all who did receive him, to those who believed in his name, he gave the right to become children of God—children born not of natural descent, nor of human decision or a husband's will, but born of God.

It begins with believing, yet *believing* can be a deceptive word. We can believe in all we have read through and considered these past twenty-five days and still be no closer to the real miracle of Christmas. We can believe Jesus is the Son of God and even the Savior of the world in the same way we believe the sky is blue and gravity is real. The birth of Jesus on Christmas Day, his resurrection on Easter, and his certain return on an unknown future date can be eternal verities we run up the flagpole and salute and yet remain unaffected in our lives by their truth. Examine the text closer:

Yet to all who did receive him, to those who believed in his name, he gave the right to become children of God . . .

Believing must lead to becoming, lest believing be emptied of its power. The whole point of Advent—indeed, of the gospel—is that seeds of faith be sown in our minds and hearts such that something genuinely and stunningly new could break through the service and burst into life.

Track further with the text:

. . . children born not of natural descent, nor of human decision or a husband's will, but born of God.

Though the language has become cliché and caricatured through the years, the Bible is clear about being "born again." Jesus said it plainly, "Very truly I tell you, no one can see the kingdom of God unless they are born again" (John 3:3 NIV).

The anonymous hymn writer may have said it best:

Though Christ a thousand times
in Bethlehem be born,
if He's not born in thee,
Thy soul is still forlorn.*

This is the invitation of Christmas: not passive belief but active becoming. It's taking the risk of new birth. As gifts are given and received and the wrapping paper gathered up, the excitement of the day will recede. As the sentimentality of the day fades, the serious possibility remains: Will you humble yourself like a child? Will you receive, believe, and be born again and become humble before the God of heaven and earth, the Lord over all creation, Jesus Christ? What could be a better story than to say you were born again on Christmas Day?

The Prayer

Our Father in heaven, nearer than my breath, thank you for these days of Advent and this new year in Christ. I want to be born again. I want to believe in Jesus in a deeper way than before. I want to receive him into the depths of my being. Lord, Jesus, I want for you to be born in me in a new and deeper way. I don't discount what has happened prior to this

---

* Author unknown, "O Cross of Christ."

day in my walk with you. I only know it has led to this present moment where I want to say yes to you like never before. I want to become one of the children of God afresh. Come, Holy Spirit, and let the life of Jesus Christ be born anew and afresh in me today and lead forward in a way of growing up in him and into the life I was made for. In the name of Jesus Messiah—the one who came, is here, and is coming again— for his glory and our good, amen.

The Questions

- How will these days of Advent unfold now into the rest of this new year in Christ for you and your family? How will this year be different? Better? More challenging?

Titles in the Seedbed Daily Text series: